T0023359

TABLE OF CONTENTS

TEXAS AND TREES

Texas is a great place for anyone interested in trees. With the *Trees of Texas Field Guide*, you'll be able to quickly identify 180 of the most common trees in Texas—most of which are native to the state. This guide also includes a number of common non-native trees that have been naturalized in Texas. This book makes no attempt to identify cultivated or nursery trees.

Because this book is a unique all-photographic field guide just for Texas, you won't have to page through photographs of trees that don't grow in the state, or attempt to identify live trees by studying black-and-white line drawings.

WHAT IS A TREE?

For the purposes of this book, a tree is defined as a large woody perennial plant, usually with a single erect trunk, standing at least 15 feet (4.5 m) tall, with a well-defined crown. *Trees of Texas Field Guide* helps you observe some basic characteristics of trees so you can identify different species confidently.

HOW THIS BOOK IS ORGANIZED

To identify a tree, you'll want to start by looking at the thumb tabs in the upper right-hand corner of the text pages. These tabs define the sections of the book. They combine several identifying features of a tree (main category, needle or leaf type and attachment) into one icon.

It's possible to identify trees using this field guide without learning about categories, leaf types and attachments. Simply flip through the pages to match your sample to the features depicted on the thumb tabs. Once you find the correct section, use the photos to find your tree. Or, you may want to learn more about the features of trees in a methodical way, using the following steps to narrow your choices to just a few photos.

1. First, determine the appropriate section and find the right icon by asking these questions: Is the tree coniferous or deciduous? If it is a conifer, are the needles single, clustered or scaly? If it is deciduous, is the leaf type simple, lobed or compound, and do leaves attach to twigs in an opposite or alternate pattern?

2. Next, simply browse through the photos in that section to find your tree. Or, to further narrow your choices, use the icon in the lower right-hand corner of the text pages. These icons are grouped by the general shape of the needle or leaf, and they increase in size as the average size of the needle or leaf increases.

3. Finally, by examining the full-page photos of needles or leaves, studying the inset photos of bark, flowers, fruit or other special features and considering information on text pages, you should be able to confidently identify the tree.

4. In addition, a special tree-like species section on pp. 384–385 includes photos and general information for 6 species of cacti and shrubs that you may mistakenly identify as a tree.

IDENTIFICATION STEP-BY-STEP
Conifer or Deciduous

Trees in this field guide are first grouped into two main categories that consist of 20 conifers and 154 deciduous trees.

Trees with evergreen needles that remain on branches year-round and have seeds in cones are conifers. Some examples of these are pines and junipers. The only exception in this main category is the Bald Cypress, a conifer that behaves like a deciduous tree, shedding its needles in the fall. Trees with broad flat leaves that fall off their branches each autumn are deciduous. Some examples of these are oaks and maples. Many deciduous trees in Texas, however, remain evergreen during winter until temperatures dip below freezing.

You will see by looking at the thumb tabs that trees with needles (conifers) are shown in the first sections of the book, followed by trees with leaves (deciduous).

Needle or Leaf Type
CONIFER GROUP:
Single, Clustered or Scaly Needles

SINGLE **CLUSTERED** **SCALY**
(Range of
2–30 needles)

If the tree is a conifer, the next step is to distinguish among single, clustered and scaly needles. Begin by checking the number of needles that arise from one point. If you see only one needle arising from one point, look in the single needle section. Conifers with single needles are shown first. If there are at least two needles arising from one point, turn to the clustered needles section. This second section is organized by the number of needles in a cluster. If you are trying to identify needles that overlap each other and have a scale-like appearance, unlike the other needles, you will find this type in the scaly needles section.

DECIDUOUS GROUP:
Simple, Lobed or Compound

SIMPLE **LOBED** **COMPOUND** **TWICE COMPOUND** **PALMATE COMPOUND**

If the tree is deciduous, the next step is to determine the leaf type. Many of the simple leaves have a basic shape such as oval, round or triangular. Other simple leaves are lobed, identified by noticeable indentations along their edges. Simple leaves without lobes are grouped first, followed by the lobed leaf groups.

If a leaf is composed of smaller leaflets growing along a single stalk, you'll find this type in the compound leaf sections. When a leaf has small leaflets growing along the edge of a thinner secondary stalk, which is in turn attached to a thicker main stalk, check the twice compound section. If the leaf has leaflets emerging from a common central point at the end of a leafstalk, look in the palmate compound section.

Leaf Attachment

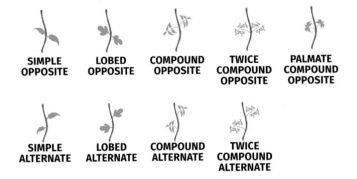

SIMPLE OPPOSITE   **LOBED OPPOSITE**   **COMPOUND OPPOSITE**   **TWICE COMPOUND OPPOSITE**   **PALMATE COMPOUND OPPOSITE**

SIMPLE ALTERNATE   **LOBED ALTERNATE**   **COMPOUND ALTERNATE**   **TWICE COMPOUND ALTERNATE**

For deciduous trees, once you have determined the appropriate leaf type, give special attention to the pattern in which the leaves are attached to the twig. Trees with leaves that attach directly opposite of each other on a twig are grouped first in each section, followed by trees with leaves that attach alternately. The thumb tabs are labeled "opposite" or "alternate" to reflect the attachment group. All the above features (main category, needle or leaf type and attachment) are depicted in one icon for easy use.

Needle or Leaf Size

Once you have found the correct section by using the thumb tabs, note that the section is further loosely organized by needle or leaf size from small to large. Size is depicted in the needle or leaf icon located in the lower right-hand corner of text pages. This icon also reflects the shape of the needle or leaf. For example, the icon for the Peachleaf Willow, which has a leaf size of 2–4 inches (5–10 cm), is smaller than the icon for the Desert Willow with a leaf size of 6–8 inches (15–20 cm). Measurement of any deciduous leaf extends from the base of the leaf (excluding the leafstalk) to the tip.

Using Photos and Icons to Confirm the Identity

After using the thumb tabs to narrow your choices, the last step is to confirm the tree's identity. First, compare the full-page photo of the leaves and twigs to be sure they look similar. Next, study the color and texture of the bark, and compare it to the inset photo. Then consider the information given about the habitat and range.

Sometimes, however, it is a special characteristic, such as flowers, fruit or thorns (described and/or pictured), that is an even better indicator of the identity. In general, if it's spring, check for flowers. During summer, look for fruit. In autumn, note the fall color.

Another icon is also included for each species to show the overall shape of the average mature tree and how its height compares with a two-story house. For trees with an average height of more than 50 feet (15 m), this icon is shown on a slightly smaller scale.

STAN'S NOTES

Stan's Notes is fun and fact-filled with many gee-whiz tidbits of interesting information, such as historical uses, other common names and much more. Most information given in this descriptive section cannot be found in other tree field guides.

CAUTION

In Stan's Notes, it's occasionally mentioned that parts of some trees were used for medicine or food. While some find this interesting, DO NOT use this field guide to identify edible or medicinal trees. Certain trees in the state have toxic properties or poisonous look-alikes that can cause severe problems. Do not take the chance of making a mistake. Please enjoy the trees of Texas with your eyes, nose or with your camera. In addition, please don't pull off leaves, cut branches or attempt to transplant any trees. Nearly all of the trees you will see are available at your local garden centers. These trees have been cultivated and have not been uprooted from the wild. Trees are an important part of our natural environment, and leaving a healthy tree unharmed will do a great deal to help keep the Lone Star State the wondrous place it is.

Enjoy the Trees!

LEAF BASICS

It's easier to identify trees and communicate about them when you know the names of the different parts of a leaf. For instance, it is more effective to use the word "sinus" to indicate an indentation on an edge of a leaf than to try to describe it.

The following illustrations show coniferous needles in cross section and the basic parts of deciduous leaves. The simple/lobed leaf and compound leaf illustrations are composites of leaves and should not be confused with any actual leaf of a real tree.

Needle Cross Sections

square   flat   triangular   round

Simple/Lobed Leaf

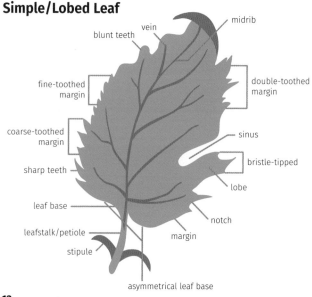

midrib

vein

blunt teeth

fine-toothed margin

double-toothed margin

coarse-toothed margin

sinus

bristle-tipped

sharp teeth

lobe

leaf base

notch

leafstalk/petiole

margin

stipule

asymmetrical leaf base

Compound Leaf

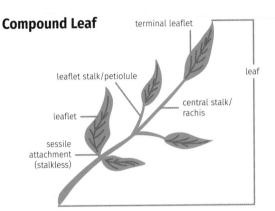

terminal leaflet

leaf

leaflet stalk/petiolule

central stalk/
rachis

leaflet

sessile
attachment
(stalkless)

FINDING YOUR TREE IN A SECTION

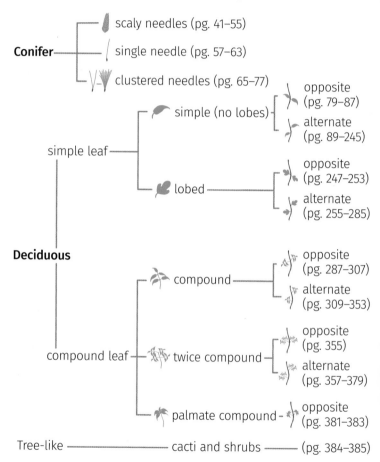

Conifer — scaly needles (pg. 41–55)
single needle (pg. 57–63)
clustered needles (pg. 65–77)

Deciduous

simple leaf —
simple (no lobes) —
opposite (pg. 79–87)
alternate (pg. 89–245)

lobed —
opposite (pg. 247–253)
alternate (pg. 255–285)

compound leaf —
compound —
opposite (pg. 287–307)
alternate (pg. 309–353)

twice compound —
opposite (pg. 355)
alternate (pg. 357–379)

palmate compound —
opposite (pg. 381–383)

Tree-like ——— cacti and shrubs ——— (pg. 384–385)

The smaller needles and leaves tend to be toward the front of each section, while larger sizes can be found toward the back. Check the icon in the lower right corner of text pages to compare relative size.

SILHOUETTE QUICK COMPARES

To quickly narrow down which mature tree you've found, compare its rough outline with the samples found here. For a sense of scale, we've included the tree's height range compared with a drawing of a typical U.S. house. Obviously, tree heights and general shapes can vary significantly across individuals, but this should help you rule out some possible options, hopefully pointing you in the right direction. Once you've found a possible match, turn to the specified page and confirm or rule it out by examining the photos of bark and leaves and the accompanying text.

Alderleaf Mountain-mahogany
5–15'
pg. 139

Hairy Mountain-mahogany
5–15'
pg. 137

Shrub Live Oak
5–15'
pg. 149

Desert Hackberry
10–15'
pg. 199

Saltcedar
10–15'
pg. 89

Bigelow Oak
10–20'
pg. 259

Catclaw Acacia
10–20'
pg. 359

Chalk Maple
10–20'
pg. 247

Chinese Privet
10–20'
pg. 79

Crab Apple
10–20'
pg. 101

Gregg Ash
10–20'
pg. 297

Honey Mesquite
10–20'
pg. 313

Leatherwood
10–20'
pg. 107

Mohr Oak
10–20'
pg. 157

New Mexico Locust
10–20'
pg. 341

One-seed Juniper
10–20'
pg. 47

Pinchot Juniper
10–20'
pg. 43

Prairie Sumac
10–20'
pg. 321

SILHOUETTE QUICK COMPARES, *continued*

Roemer Acacia
10–20'
pg. 361

Russian Olive
10–20'
pg. 99

Sand Post Oak
10–20'
pg. 261

Shining Sumac
10–20'
pg. 323

Sweet Acacia
10–20'
pg. 363

Texas Mulberry
10–20'
pg. 233

White Leadtree
10–20'
pg. 369

Knowlton Hophornbeam
10–25'
pg. 207

Rusty Blackhaw
10–25'
pg. 81

Screwbean Mesquite
10–25'
pg. 315

Texas Mountain Laurel
10–25'
pg. 317

Utah Serviceberry
10–25'
pg. 91

Chisos Red Oak
10–30'
pg. 267

Eve's Necklace
10–30'
pg. 319

Mexican Ash
10–30'
pg. 295

Mexican Blue Oak
10–30'
pg. 151

Netleaf Hackberry
10–30'
pg. 201

Rocky Mountain Juniper
10–30'
pg. 41

Texas Pistache
10–30'
pg. 289

White Mulberry
10–30'
pg. 235

Alligator Juniper
10–35'
pg. 51

Brazilian Peppertree
10–40'
pg. 293

Netleaf Oak
10–40'
pg. 153

Texas Persimmon
10–40'
pg. 211

Baretta
15–20'
pg. 287

Hercules Club
15–20'
pg. 351

Sandpaper Oak
15–20'
pg. 147

American Hornbeam
15–25'
pg. 113

Hawthorn
15–25'
pg. 109

Mexican Plum
15–25'
pg. 221

Texas Palo Verde
15–25'
pg. 309

Texas Redbud
15–25'
pg. 123

Coast Laurel Oak
15–30'
pg. 167

Southern Wax-myrtle
15–30'
pg. 105

Carolina Buckthorn
15–40'
pg. 111

Desert Willow
20–25'
pg. 231

Goldenball Leadtree
20–25'
pg. 365

Possum Haw
20–25'
pg. 143

Yaupon
20–25'
pg. 141

American Smoketree
20–30'
pg. 119

Brasil
20–30'
pg. 93

Devil's Walkingstick
20–30'
pg. 379

Flowering Dogwood
20–30'
pg. 83

Fringetree
20–30'
pg. 85

Lacey Oak
20–30'
pg. 155

Pawpaw
20–30'
pg. 135

Red Buckeye
20–30'
pg. 381

Red Mulberry
20–30'
pg. 237

SILHOUETTE QUICK COMPARES, *continued*

Saffron Plum
20–30'
pg. 183

Silktree
20–30'
pg. 377

Texas Ebony
20–30'
pg. 355

Texas Madrone
20–30'
pg. 95

Texas Olive
20–30'
pg. 131

Two-winged Silverbell
20–30'
pg. 117

Weeping Juniper
20–30'
pg. 45

Western Soapberry
20–30'
pg. 353

Wright Acacia
20–30'
pg. 357

Sweetleaf
20–35'
pg. 121

Anacua
20–40'
pg. 97

Arizona Walnut
20–40'
pg. 345

Ashe Juniper
20–40'
pg. 49

Carolina Ash
20–40'
pg. 305

Chinaberry
20–40'
pg. 375

Ironwood
20–40'
pg. 209

Laurel Cherry
20–40'
pg. 223

Mexican Palo Verde
20–40'
pg. 311

Sweetbay
20–40'
pg. 243

Texas Buckeye
20–40'
pg. 383

Silverleaf Oak
20–45'
pg. 171

Gambel Oak
25–30'
pg. 271

Blackjack Oak
25–40'
pg. 265

Arizona White Oak
25–50'
pg. 165

Black Cherry
25–50'
pg. 225

Eastern Redcedar
25–50'
pg. 55

Emory Oak
25–50'
pg. 163

Gray Oak
25–50'
pg. 161

Great Leadtree
25–50'
pg. 367

Texas Walnut
25–50'
pg. 347

Post Oak
25–60'
pg. 273

Common Persimmon
30–40'
pg. 213

Osage-orange
30–40'
pg. 127

Texas Live Oak
30–40'
pg. 159

Two-needle Pinyon
30–40'
pg. 65

Bigtooth Maple
30–50'
pg. 253

Black Locust
30–50'
pg. 343

Boxelder
30–50'
pg. 291

Chittamwood
30–50'
pg. 185

Live Oak
30–50'
pg. 173

Montezuma Bald Cypress
30–50'
pg. 59

Peachleaf Willow
30–50'
pg. 227

Siberian Elm
30–50'
pg. 187

Texas Ash
30–50'
pg. 301

Texas Red Oak
30–50'
pg. 263

Velvet Ash
30–50'
pg. 299

Water Elm
30–50'
pg. 193

Water Locust
30–50'
pg. 371

SILHOUETTE QUICK COMPARES, *continued*

Winged Elm
30–50'
pg. 191

Sassafras
30–60'
pg. 255

Mexican Pine
30–70'
pg. 69

Arizona Cypress
40–50'
pg. 53

American Holly
40–60'
pg. 145

Black Hickory
40–60'
pg. 335

Black Oak
40–60'
pg. 279

Black Willow
40–60'
pg. 229

Blue Spruce
40–60'
pg. 61

Carolina Basswood
40–60'
pg. 129

Hackberry
75–100'
pg. 203

Honey Locust
40–60'
pg. 373

Laurel Oak
40–60'
pg. 175

Overcup Oak
40–60'
pg. 283

Redbay
40–60'
pg. 125

Red Maple
40–60'
pg. 251

River Birch
40–60'
pg. 103

Shagbark Hickory
40–60'
pg. 331

Southern Sugar Maple
40–60'
pg. 249

White Ash
40–60'
pg. 307

Quaking Aspen
40–70'
pg. 215

Mockernut Hickory
40–80'
pg. 337

Green Ash
50–60'
pg. 303

Black Tupelo
50–70'
pg. 239

Cedar Elm
50–70'
pg. 189

Chinquapin Oak
50–70'
pg. 179

Douglas Fir
50–70'
pg. 63

Nutmeg Hickory
50–70'
pg. 329

Ponderosa Pine
50–70'
pg. 71

Slippery Elm
50–70'

Water Oak
50–70'
pg. 177

White Oak
50–70'
pg. 277

Black Walnut
50–75'
pg. 349

Southern Catalpa
50–75'
pg. 87

Bur Oak
50–80'
pg. 285

Southwestern White Pine
50–80'
pg. 77

Swamp Chestnut Oak
50–80'
pg. 181

Willow Oak
50–80'
pg. 169

Bitternut Hickory
50–100'
pg. 325

American Beech
60–80'
pg. 115

Nuttall Oak
60–80'
pg. 269

Pignut Hickory
60–80'
pg. 327

Southern Magnolia
60–80'
pg. 245

Southern Red Oak
60–80'
pg. 281

Sugarberry
60–80'
pg. 205

Shumard Oak
60–90'
pg. 275

Sycamore
60–90'
pg. 133

Water Hickory
70–90'
pg. 333

21

SILHOUETTE QUICK COMPARES, *continued*

American Elm
70–100'
pg. 195

**Eastern
Cottonwood**
70–100'
pg. 219

**Rio Grande
Cottonwood**
70–100'
pg. 217

Shortleaf Pine
70–100'
pg. 67

Bald Cypress
80–100'
pg. 57

Loblolly Pine
80–100'
pg. 73

Longleaf Pine
80–100'
pg. 75

Pecan
80–100'
pg. 339

Sweetgum
80–100'
pg. 257

Water Tupelo
80–100'
pg. 241

NEEDLE AND LEAF QUICK COMPARES

To help you differentiate among similar-looking tree species, compare your finds with the following leaf images. For each species, we've also included information about the leaf shape and attachment, which can help quickly point you in the right direction.

Note: Leaf images are not to scale.

Rocky Mountain Juniper
scaly needles
pg. 41

Pinchot Juniper
scaly needles
pg. 43

Weeping Juniper
scaly needles
pg. 45

One-seed Juniper
scaly needles
pg. 47

Ashe Juniper
scaly needles
pg. 49

Alligator Juniper
scaly needles
pg. 51

Arizona Cypress
scaly needles
pg. 53

Eastern Redcedar
scaly needles
pg. 55

Bald Cypress
single needle
pg. 57

Montezuma Bald Cypress
single needle
pg. 59

Blue Spruce
single needle
pg. 61

Douglas Fir
single needle
pg. 63

Two-needle Pinyon
clustered needles
pg. 65

Shortleaf Pine
clustered needles
pg. 67

Mexican Pine
clustered needles
pg. 69

Ponderosa Pine
clustered needles
pg. 71

Loblolly Pine
clustered needles
pg. 73

Longleaf Pine
clustered needles
pg. 75

Southwestern White Pine
clustered needles
pg. 77

Chinese Privet
simple opposite
pg. 79

Rusty Blackhaw
simple opposite
pg. 81

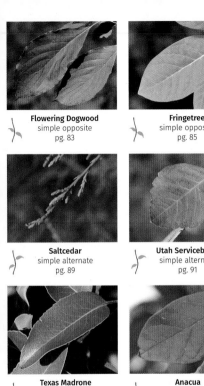

Flowering Dogwood
simple opposite
pg. 83

Fringetree
simple opposite
pg. 85

Southern Catalpa
simple opposite
pg. 87

Saltcedar
simple alternate
pg. 89

Utah Serviceberry
simple alternate
pg. 91

Brasil
simple alternate
pg. 93

Texas Madrone
simple alternate
pg. 95

Anacua
simple alternate
pg. 97

Russian Olive
simple alternate
pg. 99

Crab Apple
simple alternate
pg. 101

River Birch
simple alternate
pg. 103

Southern Wax-myrtle
simple alternate
pg. 105

Leatherwood
simple alternate
pg. 107

Hawthorn
simple alternate
pg. 109

Carolina Buckthorn
simple alternate
pg. 111

American Hornbeam
simple alternate
pg. 113

American Beech
simple alternate
pg. 115

Two-winged Silverbell
simple alternate
pg. 117

American Smoketree
simple alternate
pg. 119

Sweetleaf
simple alternate
pg. 121

Texas Redbud
simple alternate
pg. 123

Redbay
simple alternate
pg. 125

Osage-orange
simple alternate
pg. 127

Carolina Basswood
simple alternate
pg. 129

Texas Olive
simple alternate
pg. 131

Sycamore
simple alternate
pg. 133

Pawpaw
simple alternate
pg. 135

Hairy Mountain-mahogany
simple alternate
pg. 137

Alderleaf Mountain-mahogany
simple alternate
pg. 139

Yaupon
simple alternate
pg. 141

Possum Haw
simple alternate
pg. 143

American Holly
simple alternate
pg. 145

Sandpaper Oak
simple alternate
pg. 147

Shrub Live Oak
simple alternate
pg. 149

Mexican Blue Oak
simple alternate
pg. 151

Netleaf Oak
simple alternate
pg. 153

Lacey Oak
simple alternate
pg. 155

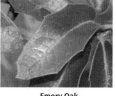
Mohr Oak
simple alternate
pg. 157

Texas Live Oak
simple alternate
pg. 159

Gray Oak
simple alternate
pg. 161

Emory Oak
simple alternate
pg. 163

Arizona White Oak
simple alternate
pg. 165

Coast Laurel Oak
simple alternate
pg. 167

Willow Oak
simple alternate
pg. 169

Silverleaf Oak
simple alternate
pg. 171

Live Oak
simple alternate
pg. 173

Laurel Oak
simple alternate
pg. 175

Water Oak
simple alternate
pg. 177

Chinquapin Oak
simple alternate
pg. 179

Swamp Chestnut Oak
simple alternate
pg. 181

Saffron Plum
simple alternate
pg. 183

Chittamwood
simple alternate
pg. 185

Siberian Elm
simple alternate
pg. 187

Cedar Elm
simple alternate
pg. 189

Winged Elm
simple alternate
pg. 191

Water Elm
simple alternate
pg. 193

American Elm
simple alternate
pg. 195

Slippery Elm
simple alternate
pg. 197

Desert Hackberry
simple alternate
pg. 199

Netleaf Hackberry
simple alternate
pg. 201

29

Hackberry
simple alternate
pg. 203

Sugarberry
simple alternate
pg. 205

Knowlton Hophornbeam
simple alternate
pg. 207

Ironwood
simple alternate
pg. 209

Texas Persimmon
simple alternate
pg. 211

Common Persimmon
simple alternate
pg. 213

Quaking Aspen
simple alternate
pg. 215

Rio Grande Cottonwood
simple alternate
pg. 217

Eastern Cottonwood
simple alternate
pg. 219

Mexican Plum
simple alternate
pg. 221

Laurel Cherry
simple alternate
pg. 223

Black Cherry
simple alternate
pg. 225

Peachleaf Willow
simple alternate
pg. 227

Black Willow
simple alternate
pg. 229

Desert Willow
simple alternate
pg. 231

Texas Mulberry
simple alternate
pg. 233

White Mulberry
simple alternate
pg. 235

Red Mulberry
simple alternate
pg. 237

Black Tupelo
simple alternate
pg. 239

Water Tupelo
simple alternate
pg. 241

Sweetbay
simple alternate
pg. 243

Southern Magnolia
simple alternate
pg. 245

Chalk Maple
lobed opposite
pg. 247

Southern Sugar Maple
lobed opposite
pg. 249

Red Maple
lobed opposite
pg. 251

Bigtooth Maple
lobed opposite
pg. 253

Sassafras
lobed alternate
pg. 255

Sweetgum
lobed alternate
pg. 257

Bigelow Oak
lobed alternate
pg. 259

Sand Post Oak
lobed alternate
pg. 261

Texas Red Oak
lobed alternate
pg. 263

Blackjack Oak
lobed alternate
pg. 265

Chisos Red Oak
lobed alternate
pg. 267

Nuttall Oak
lobed alternate
pg. 269

Gambel Oak
lobed alternate
pg. 271

Post Oak
lobed alternate
pg. 273

Shumard Oak
lobed alternate
pg. 275

White Oak
lobed alternate
pg. 277

Black Oak
lobed alternate
pg. 279

Southern Red Oak
lobed alternate
pg. 281

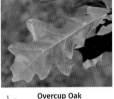

Overcup Oak
lobed alternate
pg. 283

Bur Oak
lobed alternate
pg. 285

Baretta
compound opposite
pg. 287

Texas Pistache
compound opposite
pg. 289

Boxelder
compound opposite
pg. 291

Brazilian Peppertree
compound opposite
pg. 293

Mexican Ash
compound opposite
pg. 295

Gregg Ash
compound opposite
pg. 297

Velvet Ash
compound opposite
pg. 299

Texas Ash
compound opposite
pg. 301

Green Ash
compound opposite
pg. 303

Carolina Ash
compound opposite
pg. 305

White Ash
compound opposite
pg. 307

Texas Palo Verde
compound alternate
pg. 309

Mexican Palo Verde
compound alternate
pg. 311

Honey Mesquite
compound alternate
pg. 313

Screwbean Mesquite
compound alternate
pg. 315

Texas Mountain Laurel
compound alternate
pg. 317

Eve's Necklace
compound alternate
pg. 319

Prairie Sumac
compound alternate
pg. 321

Shining Sumac
compound alternate
pg. 323

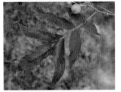
Bitternut Hickory
compound alternate
pg. 325

Pignut Hickory
compound alternate
pg. 327

Nutmeg Hickory
compound alternate
pg. 329

Shagbark Hickory
compound alternate
pg. 331

Water Hickory
compound alternate
pg. 333

Black Hickory
compound alternate
pg. 335

Mockernut Hickory
compound alternate
pg. 337

Pecan
compound alternate
pg. 339

New Mexico Locust
compound alternate
pg. 341

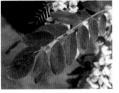
Black Locust
compound alternate
pg. 343

Arizona Walnut
compound alternate
pg. 345

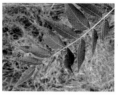

Texas Walnut
compound alternate
pg. 347

Black Walnut
compound alternate
pg. 349

Hercules Club
compound alternate
pg. 351

Western Soapberry
compound alternate
pg. 353

Texas Ebony
twice compound
opposite
pg. 355

Wright Acacia
twice compound
alternate
pg. 357

Catclaw Acacia
twice compound
alternate
pg. 359

Roemer Acacia
twice compound
alternate
pg. 361

Sweet Acacia
twice compound
alternate
pg. 363

Goldenball Leadtree
twice compound
alternate
pg. 365

Great Leadtree
twice compound
alternate
pg. 367

White Leadtree
twice compound
alternate
pg. 369

Water Locust
twice compound
alternate
pg. 371

Honey Locust
twice compound
alternate
pg. 373

Chinaberry
twice compound
alternate
pg. 375

Silktree
twice compound
alternate
pg. 377

Devil's Walkingstick
twice compound
alternate
pg. 379

Red Buckeye
palmate compound
opposite
pg. 381

Texas Buckeye
palmate compound
opposite
pg. 383

underside

bark

flower

fruit

Common Name

Scientific name

Family: common family name (scientific family name)

Height: average range in feet and meters of the mature tree from ground to top of crown

Tree: overall description; may include a shape, type of trunk, branches or crown

Leaf/Needle: type of leaf or needle, shape, size, and attachment; may include lobes, leaflets, margin, veins, color or leafstalk

Bark: color and texture of the trunk; may include inner bark or thorns

Flower: catkin, flower; may include shape, size or color

Fruit/Cone: seed, nut, berry; may include shape, size, or color

Fall Color: color(s) that deciduous leaves turn to in autumn

Origin/Age: native or non-native to the state; average life span

Habitat: type of soil, places found, sun or shade tolerance

Range: throughout or part of Texas where the tree is found; may include places where planted

Stan's Notes: Helpful identification information, history, origin and other interesting gee-whiz nature facts.

Shape of an individual needle, needle cluster, or leaf. Use this icon to compare relative size among similarly shaped leaves.

bark

cone

Rocky Mountain Juniper
Juniperus scopulorum

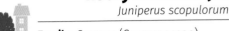

Family: Cypress (Cupressaceae)

Height: 10–30' (3–9.1 m)

Tree: pyramid shape with a single short stout trunk and branching to the ground, shorter and much wider in open areas, dense pointed crown

Needle: scaly needles, ½–1" (1–2.5 cm) long, made of tiny scale-like needles, ⅛" (.3 cm) long, that slightly overlap each other, each with a pointed tip, pale green to gray green

Bark: reddish brown, thin and fibrous, becoming gray and peeling into long narrow shreds with age

Cone: green, turning bright blue at maturity, often with a whitish cast, appearing berry-like, ¼" (.6 cm) wide, thin skin, contains 1–2 seeds, matures in 2 seasons

Origin/Age: native; 300–500 years

Habitat: dry sandy soils from 2,000–6,000' (610–1,830 m), open hillsides, rocky bluffs, sun

Range: northern quarter of Texas into the panhandle

Stan's Notes: Fairly uncommon in Texas. Isolated in the panhandle and western Texas, but can be common in western states. Found in higher elevations of the Guadalupe Mountains and lower elevations of surrounding areas. A slow grower, often scattered among other tree species. Sometimes in pure stands. Trees may be male or female (dioecious), and the seed cones grow only on female trees. Produces some cones annually, with good cone crops every 3–5 years. Wild Turkeys, Mule Deer and other large animals eat the cones. Closely related to the Eastern Redcedar (pg. 55), but Rocky Mountain cones take twice as long to mature. Hybridizes with Eastern Redcedar where ranges overlap. Also called Rocky Mountain Cedar or Western Redcedar. Wood has been used in fence posts.

bark

cone

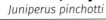
Pinchot Juniper
Juniperus pinchotti

Family: Cypress (Cupressaceae)

Height: 10–20' (3–6.1 m)

Tree: shrub to small tree with many irregular bent trunks and an irregular crown

Needle: scaly needles, ½–1" (1–2.5 cm) long, made of many tiny scale-like needles, ⅛" (.3 cm) long, that overlap each other, each broadest at the base, tapering to a sharply pointed tip, yellowish green

Bark: reddish brown, thin and shaggy

Cone: green, turning bright red when mature, round, appearing berry-like, ¼–⅓" (.6–.8 cm) wide, maturing in 1 season

Origin/Age: native; 200–500 years

Habitat: sandy soils, clay soils, canyons, mesas, hillsides, full sun

Range: western half of Texas

Stan's Notes: A small tree, often shrub-like, usually found in large groups. Due to its multiple trunks, low growth and propensity for individuals to grow close together, it often forms thick stands. Can reach a height of 20 feet (6.1 m) when growing alone, but in large groups it usually does not get above 10 feet (3 m). Resprouts from stumps after being cut or burned. Trunks that sprout after cutting or burning often grow lower to the ground, which helps produce large low stands. Because of the low growth, the wood is not used for much other than fence posts. Also called Redberry Juniper for its bright red cones or "berries," which mature in the fall of each year. Seen in rocky canyons and on hillsides in western Texas.

bark

cone

Weeping Juniper
Juniperus flaccida

Family: Cypress (Cupressaceae)

Height: 20–30' (6.1–9.1 m)

Tree: small tree with a single trunk and many drooping branches, wide flattened or rounded crown

Needle: scaly needles, ½–1" (1–2.5 cm) long, made of many tiny scale-like needles, ⅛" (.3 cm) long, that overlap each other, each broadest at the base, tapering to a sharply pointed tip, light green to yellowish green

Bark: reddish brown, shredding into narrow long strips when young, becoming thick with long flattened plates with age

Cone: green, turning red at maturity, round, covered in a whitish powdery coating, appearing berry-like, ¼–½" (.6–1 cm) wide, containing 4–12 seeds, maturing in 1 season

Origin/Age: native; 300–600 years

Habitat: rocky and sandy soils at 5,000' (1,525 m), pine and oak woodlands, canyons, hillsides, full sun

Range: Big Bend National Park

Stan's Notes: Big Bend National Park is the only place in Texas and the country where this very slow-growing, long-lived tree occurs naturally. Often associated with pine and oak forests. The largest of these trees is in Juniper Canyon and is easily distinguished from the other junipers by its drooping (pendant) branches and branchlets. Produces cones annually, with large seed crops every 3–5 years. Cones grow only on female trees (dioecious) and tend to be slightly larger and more obvious than on the other juniper species. The main population of this tree is found in the mountains of Mexico, where it is the most common juniper.

bark

cone

One-seed Juniper
Juniperus monosperma

Family: Cypress (Cupressaceae)

Height: 10–20' (3–6.1 m)

Tree: compact, often round small tree to large shrub, single trunk dividing into multiple trunks, dense foliage often obscuring the trunks, broad irregular crown

Needle: scaly needles, ½–1½" (1–4 cm) long, made of tiny scale-like needles, ⅛" (.3 cm) long, that overlap each other, each with a sharply pointed tip, dark green

Bark: gray, thin and fibrous when young, peeling into long narrow shreds with age

Cone: green, turning dark blue to copper-colored with a whitish cast when mature, appearing berry-like, ¼" (.6 cm) wide, contains 1 seed, matures in 2 seasons

Origin/Age: native; 300–600 years

Habitat: dry sandy soils, open hillsides, full sun

Range: scattered in the northern quarter of Texas, mainly in the panhandle

Stan's Notes: Grows in low to medium elevations. Usually is under 20 feet (6.1 m) tall, but some in Texas reach 30 feet (9.1 m). Much more common in New Mexico and Arizona than in Texas. Male and female flowers grow on separate trees (dioecious), resulting in cone production in the female trees only. The common name "One-seed" refers to its single seed per cone. Also called Cherrystone Juniper and West Texas Juniper.

bark

cone

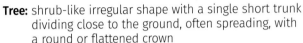

Ashe Juniper
Juniperus ashei

Family: Cypress (Cupressaceae)

Height: 20–40' (6.1–12.2 m)

Tree: shrub-like irregular shape with a single short trunk dividing close to the ground, often spreading, with a round or flattened crown

Needle: scaly needles, ½–1½" (1–4 cm) long, made of tiny scale-like needles, ⅛" (.3 cm) long, that overlap each other, each broadest at the base, tapering to a sharply pointed tip, bluish green

Bark: gray to reddish brown and thin, shredding into thin long ridges

Cone: green, turning light blue (sometimes black) when mature, broadest at the base, covered with a whitish cast, appearing berry-like, ¼–⅓" (.6–.8 cm) wide, containing 1 seed

Origin/Age: native; 300–600 years

Habitat: sandy soils, open hillsides, canyons, near water, full sun to partial shade

Range: northern and central Texas

Stan's Notes: Large shrub to small tree, native to Texas, Oklahoma and Arkansas. Occurs at lower altitudes on limestone hills, sometimes forming large thickets. Once seen only in Texas in regions protected from fires, but after settlement and fire control, the species found its way out into less protected areas of the state. Many bird species gather the long narrow strips of bark for nesting material. The leaves have a cedar aroma when crushed. Male and female flowers grow on separate trees (dioecious), with cones found only on the female trees. Also called Mountain Cedar, Rock Cedar and Post Cedar.

cone

bark

Alligator Juniper
Juniperus deppeana

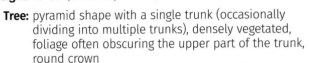

Family: Cypress (Cupressaceae)

Height: 10–35' (3–10.7 m)

Tree: pyramid shape with a single trunk (occasionally dividing into multiple trunks), densely vegetated, foliage often obscuring the upper part of the trunk, round crown

Needle: scaly needles, ½–1½" (1–4 cm) long, made of tiny scale-like needles, ⅛" (.3 cm) long, that overlap each other, each broadest at the base, tapering to a sharply pointed tip, bluish green

Bark: dark gray to nearly black, thick, deeply furrowed into neat rows of checkered squares

Cone: green, turning reddish brown (sometimes blue) at maturity, covered with a whitish cast, appearing berry-like, ¼–½" (.6–1 cm) wide, containing 2–4 seeds, maturing in 2 seasons

Origin/Age: native; 300–600 years

Habitat: sandy soils, open hillsides, canyons, near water, full sun to partial shade

Range: scattered in the Trans-Pecos region only

Stan's Notes: A handsome tree, large for a juniper. Named for the appearance of its bark. Easily identified by the unique rows of bark squares, which resemble alligator hide. Often associated with oaks and pinyon pines. Seen mostly in medium elevations. Range extends from western Texas across New Mexico and into Arizona, dipping into Mexico. Slow growing, but long lived. Produces seeds annually; can be cyclic. Many bird species, bears, squirrels and more eat the seeds. Wood is soft, brittle, light reddish and not used commercially except for fence posts. Also called Checkerbark Juniper, Western Juniper or Thickbark Juniper.

cone

bark

Arizona Cypress
Cupressus arizonica

Family: Cypress (Cupressaceae)

Height: 40–50' (12.2–15 m)

Tree: conical tree with a single straight trunk and many branches along the entire length, longer branches at the bottom, pointed (pyramidal) crown

Needle: scaly needles, ½–1" (1–2.5 cm) long, composed of many leaflets joined at the base, each ⅛" (.3 cm) long, overlapping and pressed closely to the stalk, sharp and pointed, waxy appearance, gray green, blue green or silver, aromatic

Bark: gray and thin when young, becoming reddish brown with long, narrow loose strips with age

Cone: green, round, 1" (2.5 cm) diameter, turning gray, woody and maturing in 2 years, 6–8 scales peel back to release seeds, stays on the tree many years

Origin/Age: native; 50–100 years

Habitat: rocky and sandy soils between 3,000–8,500' (915–2,590 m), canyons, ravines, slopes, sun

Range: Chisos Mountains in Big Bend National Park, planted throughout Texas in parks and yards

Stan's Notes: This species is by far the most planted tree across the state. A slow-growing, short-lived, medium-size tree with variable-colored silver-to-gray to blue-to-green needles. Needles are fragrant when crushed. Does not do well in low desert regions; usually found above 3,000 feet (915 m). Very similar to a cultivated variety (*C. glabra*), which does better in warmer, drier habitats and lower elevations. Cultivated varieties are sometimes grown as Christmas trees in southwestern states. In favorable habitats in the wild, this species grows in pure stands. Trees growing where water is more abundant grow faster.

Southern Redcedar

cone

bark

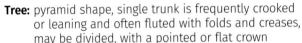

Eastern Redcedar
Juniperus virginiana

Family: Cypress (Cupressaceae)

Height: 25–50' (7.6–15 m)

Tree: pyramid shape, single trunk is frequently crooked or leaning and often fluted with folds and creases, may be divided, with a pointed or flat crown

Needle: scaly needles, 1–2" (2.5–5 cm) long, made of scale-like needles, ⅛" (.3 cm) long, that overlap each other, each with a sharply pointed tip, dark green

Bark: reddish brown to gray, thin and fibrous, peeling with age into long narrow shreds, reddish inner bark is smooth

Cone: dark blue with a white powdery film, appearing berry-like, ½" (1 cm) long, containing 1–2 seeds

Fall Color: reddish brown during winter

Origin/Age: native; 300–500 years

Habitat: dry sandy or clay soils, open hillsides, sun

Range: eastern and north central Texas, planted in yards

Stan's Notes: One of the first trees to grow back in fields after a fire. Slow growing, producing what appear to be blue berries, which are actually cones. Cones are used to flavor gin during the distillation process. Many bird species spread seeds by eating cones, dispersing seeds in their droppings. Redcedar wood is aromatic and lightweight. Often used to make storage chests, lending its scent to linens. The smooth reddish inner bark was called baton rouge or red stick by early French settlers who found the tree in Louisiana. Affected by cedar-apple rust, which causes large jelly-like orange growths. Its sharply pointed leaves can cause skin irritation. Also called Eastern Juniper or Red Juniper. Southern Redcedar (*J. v. silicicola*) (see inset), a subspecies of the Eastern, is scattered in eastern coastal Texas.

bark

cone

knees

Bald Cypress
Taxodium distichum

Family: Bald Cypress (Taxodiaceae)

Height: 80–100' (24–30 m)

Tree: large conical tree, enlarged straight trunk with a flared base (buttress) spreading into ridges, wide spreading branches, crown often pointed

Needle: single needle, ½–¾" (1–2 cm) long, in 2 rows on slender green twigs, pointed tip, soft and flexible, feather-like, yellowish green above, whitish below

Bark: brown to gray, with fibrous ridges, peeling in strips

Cone: green, turning gray to brown when mature, ¾–1" (2–2.5 cm) wide, solitary or in small clusters at the end of branch, several 4–sided woody cone scales

Fall Color: brown

Origin/Age: native; 500–750 years

Habitat: wet soils, can grow in dry upland soils, swamps, river bottoms, sun to partial shade

Range: scattered in the eastern third of Texas, Gulf Marshes

Stan's Notes: Called "Bald" since it's a deciduous conifer, losing its leaves (needles) in fall, growing new ones in spring. Produces a large flaring or fluted base, which helps stabilize it in soft wet soils. Also grows in well-drained soils, but thrives in wetter areas. Large aboveground or water growths, called knees (see inset), grow at the base of the tree, sometimes as far away as 25 feet (7.6 m) from the trunk. Long-lived, some over 1,000 years old are among the oldest living things in North America. Often called the Sequoia of the East, reaching over 100 feet (30 m) tall and nearly 40 feet (12.2 m) around the base. Ranges from Illinois to the East coast, south to Florida and west to Texas. Decay- and insect-resistant wood is used to build boats and bridges. Seeds are a food for wildlife such as ducks and deer.

bark

Montezuma Bald Cypress
Taxodium mucronatum

Family: Bald Cypress (Taxodiaceae)

Height: 30–50' (9.1–15 m)

Tree: medium-size evergreen, enlarged straight trunk with a flared base (buttress) spreading into ridges, wide spreading branches and drooping terminal branches (branchlets), crown often pointed

Needle: single needle, ½–¾" (1–2 cm) long, in 2 rows on slender green twigs, pointed at the tip, soft and flexible to touch, appearing feather-like, yellowish green above, whitish below

Bark: brown to gray, with narrow fibrous ridges, peeling off in long strips

Cone: green, turning gray to brown with age, ¾" (2 cm) wide, solitary or in small clusters at the end of the branch, several 4–sided woody cone scales

Origin/Age: native; 750–1,000 years

Habitat: wet soils, swamps, by slow rivers that flood often, sun to partial shade

Range: far southern tip of Texas in the Rio Grande Valley

Stan's Notes: Closely related to the Bald Cypress (pg. 57), but the Montezuma Bald Cypress has a limited range and strongly drooping branchlets. Found in Texas only in the extreme southern tip in two counties, Cameron and Hidalgo. Ranges from Guatemala throughout Mexico, just touching the United States in southern Texas. Not known in the United States prior to its discovery in 1926. Unlike the Bald Cypress, it does not do well as a landscape tree, is not cold tolerant and has difficulty surviving winters farther north than San Antonio. A long-lived tree, some over 1,000 years old are among the oldest living things in North America. Large aboveground or water growths, called knees, grow at the base of the tree.

bark

cone

Blue Spruce
Picea pungens

SINGLE
NEEDLE

Family: Pine (Pinaceae)

Height: 40–60' (12.2–18 m)

Tree: pyramid shape, lower branches are the widest and often touch the ground

Needle: single needle, ½–1" (1–2.5 cm) long, very stiff, very sharp point on the end, square in cross section, bluish green to silver blue

Bark: grayish brown and flaky, becoming reddish brown and deeply furrowed with age

Cone: straw-colored, 2–4" (5–10 cm) long, in clusters or single, hanging down

Origin/Age: non-native; 150–200 years (some reach 600 years)

Habitat: variety of soils, does best in clay and well-drained moist soils, sun

Range: northern half of Texas, planted in cities, parks, along roads and around homes

Stan's Notes: This is a common Christmas tree and landscaping tree that is widely planted around homes and along city streets in medium to high elevations. A victim of the Spruce Budworm and needle fungus, so not planted as much anymore. Very susceptible to cytospora canker, which invades stressed trees, causing loss of branches and eventual death. Will grow in a wide variety of soils, but prefers moist, well-drained earth. Does not do well in alkaline soils in northern Texas. Slow growing, some living up to 600 years. Needles are very sharp and square in cross section. Species name *pungens* is Latin for "sharp-pointed." Also called Colorado Spruce or Silver Spruce.

immature
cone

bark

cone

Douglas Fir

Pseudotsuga menziesii glauca

Family: Pine (Pinaceae)

Height: 50–70' (15–21 m)

Tree: scraggly-looking tree, pyramid shape, many lower branches dead and remaining on the tree, pointed irregular crown

Needle: single needle, 1–1½" (2.5–4 cm) long, arranged spirally on a twig, borne from a raised stalk, soft, linear but often curved, sharp point on the end, flat in cross section, yellow green above, two lines of white dots below

Bark: gray to brown in color with many flaky scales and scattered resin blisters (pitch pockets)

Cone: green, turning brown or straw-colored at maturity, large and distinct, 2–4" (5–10 cm) long, with curly 3–pronged cone scales, hanging from branch

Origin/Age: native; 150–200 years

Habitat: well-drained moist soils above elevations of 6,000' (1,830 m), cool shady places

Range: Guadalupe and Chisos Mountains

Stan's Notes: Found only in the pine forests and steep canyon walls of the Guadalupe Mountains above 6,000 feet (1,830 m). Also in the Chisos Mountains between 6,000–7,000 feet (1,830–2,135 m). The Texas variety of this tree is different from one found on the Pacific coast. Has very characteristic large cones with distinctive three-point cone scales. Tolerates growing in thick stands. Also called Common Douglas Fir or Blue Douglas Fir. Only two species of the genus *Pseudotsuga* are native to the western North America; the others are native to Asia. *Pseudotsuga* means "false hemlock," referring to its close resemblance to Eastern Hemlock (not shown).

bark

cone

Two-needle Pinyon

Pinus edulis

Family: Pine (Pinaceae)

Height: 30–40' (9.1–12.2 m)

Tree: single short trunk that can twist and bend, divided low with branches close to the ground, sometimes keeps dead branches for many years, widely spreading irregular crown

Needle: clustered needles, 2 per cluster (rarely 3 or 1), ½–2" (1–5 cm) long, each needle is stiff, pointed, curved toward the branch, round or triangular in cross section, bluish green

Bark: gray to reddish brown with irregular furrows and small scaly ridges

Cone: green, turning yellowish brown at maturity, ovate to round, 1½–2" (4–5 cm) long, wide and flattened when open, stalkless, sometimes on a short stalk, 2 very large, edible seeds under each cone scale

Origin/Age: native; 200–500 years

Habitat: well-drained limestone soils and dry rocky soils above 6,000' (1,830 m), slopes, sun

Range: only in the Guadalupe Mountains in Culberson County and Sierra Diablo in Hudspeth County

Stan's Notes: This western tree reaches its eastern limits in Texas. Widespread, covering nearly 61 million acres (24.4 million ha) from Texas to California. Found in the woodlands of the Guadalupe Mountains. A slow-growing tree, long lived and drought resistant. Produces cones yearly, with large crops every 3–4 years. Many bird and mammal species feed on the seeds. Seeds were a staple food of the Navajo Indians and are collected and shipped worldwide now for use by gourmet cooks. Also called Nut Pine, Colorado Pinyon, Two-leaf Pinyon or just Pinyon.

immature
cone

bark

cone

Shortleaf Pine
Pinus echinata

Family: Pine (Pinaceae)

Height: 70–100' (21–30 m)

Tree: large tree, single straight trunk, many horizontal branches, older trees often lack branches on lower half, round crown

Needle: clustered needles, 2 or 3 per cluster, 2¾–4½" (7–11 cm) long, each needle is soft, flexible, slender, sharply pointed, yellowish green

Bark: reddish brown with large, irregular flat scales

Cone: yellowish green, turning light brown at maturity, oblong, tapers near tip, 1½–2½" (4–6 cm) long, short stalk, thin cone scale, small prickle at the tip

Origin/Age: native; 100–150 years

Habitat: sandy and gravelly soils on south-facing slopes and ridges, abandoned farms, sun

Range: eastern quarter of Texas

Stan's Notes: This is one of the fastest growing pines. After cutting or fires, it quickly reestablishes with many seedlings and suckering shoots, which is uncommon for pines. Often in pure stands or with other pines. It has hard, strong, yellow-to-orange wood and is an important commercial tree, producing lumber, millwork, veneer, pulpwood and flooring. The wood is often sold as Southern Yellow Pine. Known by other names such as Shortstraw Pine, Soft Pine, Arkansas Pine and Bull Pine. Turpentine is produced from the resin. This tree has the shortest needles of the major southern yellow pines, hence the common name "Shortleaf." Reaches cone-bearing maturity at 20–30 years. Seeds look like small maple seeds and can be carried by the wind as far as a quarter mile. Widespread in the southeastern United States and native in more than 20 states.

bark

cone

Mexican Pine
Pinus cembroides

Family: Pine (Pinaceae)

Height: 30–70' (9.1–21 m)

Tree: medium tree, single thick trunk with horizontal branching, branches concentrating near the top, narrow pointed (pyramidal) crown

Needle: clustered needles, 3 (sometimes 2) per cluster, ¾–1¾" (2–4.5 cm) long, each needle is short, thin, soft and flexible, dark bluish green

Bark: gray to brown and smooth when young, breaking with age into large broad scales, separated by deep furrows

Cone: green, turning brown at maturity, round to oblong, 3–4" (7.5–10 cm) long, with a thick dark brown nutshell, edible nut, thick round cone scales

Origin/Age: native; 150–250 years

Habitat: dry, sandy and rocky soils at 4,000–6,000' (1,220–1,830 m), oak, pine and juniper forests, sun

Range: scattered in a few counties in far southwestern Texas, southern mountains in the Trans-Pecos

Stan's Notes: A pine of the mountains in the southern Trans-Pecos region above 4,000 feet (1,220 m). Identified by its short, flexible thin needles in small clusters of three or two; in some areas most have two-needle clusters. Compared with similar trees it has one of the thickest nutshells. Most wildlife and also Indigenous peoples eat the nuts. A common species in Mexico, reaching its northern limit in Texas. Often called Mexican Pinyon, Pinyon Pine or just Pinyon.

immature
cone

bark

cone

resin

Ponderosa Pine
Pinus ponderosa

Family: Pine (Pinaceae)

Height: 50–70' (15–21 m)

Tree: single straight trunk, showing little tapering, loses lower branches when mature, irregular crown

Needle: clustered needles, 3 per cluster (occasionally 2 or 5 per cluster on the same tree), 5–8" (13–20 cm) long, each needle is straight, flexible, bending rather than breaking, dark green

Bark: reddish brown with large, long black furrows and some scales

Cone: green, turning brown at maturity, 2–6" (5–15 cm) long, each cone scale armed with a sharp spine

Origin/Age: native; 150–200 years

Habitat: wide variety of soils at elevations above 5,000' (1,525 m), ridges, slopes, sun

Range: scattered in far western Texas in the Guadalupe, Davis and Chisos Mountains

Stan's Notes: One of the most widely distributed pine tree in North America and the most abundant pine in the western United States. Western Texas marks its eastern distribution. Called Western Yellow Pine before 1932. Also called Blackjack Pine. Produces a long straight trunk that is used in the lumber industry for making window sashes, paneling and cabinets. Trunks were once used for telephone poles, shoring up mine ceilings and lumber for construction. One of the few pines with two or three (rarely five) needles per cluster. Pieces of fallen bark lay at the base of the tree like jigsaw puzzle pieces. Fast growing, with a thick bark that makes the mature tree fire resistant. Cone seeds are eaten by birds and small animals. Deer eat the twigs and needles. Twigs and cones often ooze a clear, fragrant sticky sap resin (see inset) that is hard to remove from skin or clothing.

bark

cone

Loblolly Pine
Pinus taeda

Family: Pine (Pinaceae)

Height: 80–100' (24–30 m)

Tree: large tree, single straight trunk, broad round crown

Needle: clustered needles, 3 per cluster, 6–9" (15–23 cm) long, each needle is long, slender, often twisted, green to yellowish green

Bark: black to dark gray when young, turning reddish brown with scaly ridges with age, resinous and fragrant

Cone: green, turning brown at maturity, ovate, 3–5" (7.5–13 cm) long, stalkless, each cone scale is raised with a short stout spine at the tip

Origin/Age: native; 100–150 years

Habitat: variety of soils from wet to dry, river bottoms, sun

Range: eastern quarter of Texas, planted in parks, yards and pure stands

Stan's Notes: The most common and widespread pine in Texas. A native tree of the southeastern United States, ranging across more than a dozen states, finding its western limit in Texas. An extremely fast-growing species that gets very tall. Self-pruning (lower branches fall off as it grows) and develops a straight trunk, making it valuable for lumber. This is the most commercially important wild pine tree in Texas, with several varieties developed from it. Planted in pure stands as a crop tree for pulpwood and lumber, and also introduced to other continents. Common name "Loblolly" means "mud puddle" and accurately describes the wet soils the tree prefers. Also called Rosemary Pine due to its fragrance, Bull Pine because of its large trunk and Oldfield Pine since it grows in old fields.

bark

cone

Longleaf Pine
Pinus palustris

Family: Pine (Pinaceae)

Height: 80–100' (24–30 m)

Tree: large tree, single trunk with few branches, open irregular crown

Needle: clustered needles, 3 per cluster, 8–18" (20–45 cm) long, each needle is long, flexible, often twisted, bright green

Bark: orange to brown, thin with scaly plates

Cone: green, turning brown at maturity, cylindrical, 6–10" (15–25 cm) long, nearly stalkless, each cone scale has a short stout spine at the tip

Origin/Age: native; 100–150 years, some over 400 years

Habitat: dry sandy soils, sun

Range: handful of counties in far eastern Texas, planted in parks and yards

Stan's Notes: Once seen in large numbers in about six counties in far eastern Texas, but it is believed that virgin stands no longer exist. Longleaf Pine can be a long-lived tree, reaching 400 years and more. Old-growth Longleaf Pines are one of the preferred habitats of the Red-cockaded Woodpecker, an endangered bird that nests in cavities excavated in trunks of living pines. The rarity of pure old-growth stands is the primary reason for the decline of this bird. An extremely valuable commercial tree, yielding some of the best lumber on the market, with turpentine produced from the resin. Also known as Longstraw Pine, Southern Yellow Pine, Yellow Pine or Georgia Pine.

bark

young bark

cone

Southwestern White Pine
Pinus strobiformis

Family: Pine (Pinaceae)

Height: 50–80' (15–24 m)

Tree: medium to large tree, single thick trunk, evenly spaced horizontal branching along the trunk with branches concentrating near the top when mature, irregular pointed crown

Needle: clustered needles, 5 per cluster, 2½–3½" (6–9 cm) long, each needle is soft, flexible and triangular in cross section

Bark: gray to brown and smooth when young (see inset), breaking with age into large broad scales that are separated by deep furrows

Cone: green, turning brown when mature, elongated, drooping and curved, 6–10" (15–25 cm) long, pointed white tip on each cone scale, scales bend backward when open, large seeds

Origin/Age: native; 100–250 years

Habitat: dry sandy soils, upland sites, high forests, slopes, canyons, sun

Range: 1–2 counties in far western Texas, Guadalupe and Davis Mountains

Stan's Notes: A pine species of high mountain forests, occurring on dry rocky slopes and canyons. This is a medium to large native tree, not common anywhere in its range. Found mainly in the mountains of western Mexico. Seeds in cones are large and eaten by wildlife. Some Indigenous peoples collect the seeds for food.

mature fruit

immature fruit

bark

flower

Chinese Privet
Ligustrum sinense

Family: Olive (Oleaceae)

Height: 10–20' (3–6.1 m)

Tree: small tree to large shrub, multiple thin trunks, well-branched dense round crown

Leaf: simple, oval to elliptical, 1–2½" (2.5–6 cm) long, oppositely attached, leaves often appear to grow in 2 rows, toothless margin, dull green above, paler below with many fine hairs

Bark: gray, smooth

Flower: 4–petaled, bell-shaped white flower, ¼" (.6 cm) in diameter, in abundant clusters, 1–4" (2.5–10 cm) long, usually broader at the base and tapering to a point, at the end of branch, sweet fragrance

Fruit: green berry-like fleshy fruit (drupe), turning dark blue to purple at maturity, round, ¼" (.6 cm) wide, containing 1 hard seed

Fall Color: semi-evergreen

Origin/Age: non-native, introduced from China; 25–50 years

Habitat: dry to damp soils, disturbed soils, understory of woodlands, along fencerows and streams, shade

Range: planted in parks and yards

Stan's Notes: This is perhaps the largest invasive, exotic species causing problems in Texas. Introduced from China as an ornamental shrub. There are several non-native privet species, but Chinese Privet is the most aggressive and troublesome. Many species of birds eat the berry-like fruit and deposit the seeds across the region, spreading it even more. Often found in the understory of moist forests. Almost nothing can grow under it since the area is so densely shaded. Twigs as well as the underside of leaves have numerous fine hairs.

bark

flower

fruit

Rusty Blackhaw
Viburnum rufidulum

SIMPLE OPPOSITE

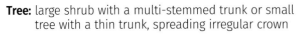

Family: Honeysuckle (Caprifoliaceae)

Height: 10–25' (3–7.6 m)

Tree: large shrub with a multi-stemmed trunk or small tree with a thin trunk, spreading irregular crown

Leaf: simple, oval, 1–3" (2.5–7.5 cm) long, oppositely attached, rounded tip, fine-toothed margin, shiny dark green above, paler with rusty hairs below (especially when young), on a ½" (1 cm) long leafstalk (petiole) covered with rusty hairs

Bark: gray and smooth when young, becoming blocky and furrowed with age

Flower: 5–petaled white flower, ¼" (.6 cm) wide, in flat clusters, 2–3" (5–7.5 cm) wide

Fruit: green berry-like fruit (drupe), turning red, then blue to black when mature, sweet and edible, round to slightly flattened, ¼–½" (.6–1 cm) wide, in clusters on a reddish fruit stalk, containing 1 seed

Fall Color: red to reddish purple

Origin/Age: native; 25–30 years

Habitat: wide variety of soils from wet to dry, along forest edges, understory in woodlands, shade or full sun

Range: eastern half of Texas, several isolated populations in the Davis Mountains in western Texas

Stan's Notes: Over 100 *Viburnum* species in the world, with more than 20 native to North America. Also called Nannyberry, Southern Blackhaw or Viburnum. White flower clusters cover it in spring, making it pretty in landscapes, followed by clusters of fruit. Fruit is hard to eat due to its large seed. Ripe fruit is a favorite of wildlife.

bark

flower

mature fruit

immature fruit

Flowering Dogwood
Cornus florida

Family: Dogwood (Cornaceae)

Height: 20–30' (6.1–9.1 m)

Tree: small tree with single trunk, spreading horizontal branches, broad flat-topped crown

Leaf: simple, oval to round, 2–5" (5–13 cm) long, oppositely attached, smooth toothless margin, deeply curving (arcuate) parallel veins, medium green above and nearly hairless, paler below and covered with fine hairs

Bark: reddish brown, broken into small square plates

Flower: several tiny green flowers, ½" (1 cm) long, crowded together and surrounded by 4 creamy white bracts, 1–2" (2.5–5 cm) long, appearing before the leaves in spring

Fruit: green berry-like fruit (drupe), turning red when mature, ¼–½" (.6–1 cm) diameter, several together on a long fruit stalk, each containing 1–2 seeds

Fall Color: red

Origin/Age: native; 30–50 years

Habitat: moist soils, forest edges, meadows, shade

Range: eastern quarter of Texas, planted in parks, yards

Stan's Notes: Early blooming of showy flowers makes this one of the most beautiful flowering trees in eastern Texas. Fruit is eaten by many bird species. Its hard wood is used to make mallet handles and heads. Red dye was once extracted from the roots. Often planted as an ornamental for its flowers and bright red fall foliage, and as food for wildlife. Because daggers were made from its wood, common name "Daggerwood" may have been slightly changed to "Dogwood." Also called Florida Dogwood, Virginia Dogwood or Eastern Dogwood.

bark

Fringetree
Chionanthus virginicus

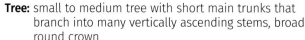

Family: Olive (Oleaceae)

Height: 20–30' (6.1–9.1 m)

Tree: small to medium tree with short main trunks that branch into many vertically ascending stems, broad round crown

Leaf: simple, 4–8" (10–20 cm) long, oppositely attached, narrowly elliptical, toothless, dark green above, paler below and sometimes covered with tiny hairs, on a short purplish leafstalk (petiole)

Bark: brown, thin with reddish brown scales

Flower: thin white flower with tiny purple dots, 1" (2.5 cm) long, hanging in clusters, 4–8" (10–20 cm) long, fragrant scent

Fruit: green berry-like fruit (drupe), turning nearly black when mature, ovate, ½–¾" (1–2 cm) wide

Fall Color: yellow

Origin/Age: native; 50–75 years

Habitat: moist soils, sandy soils, river valleys, understory of coniferous forests, shade tolerant

Range: extreme eastern Texas, Pineywoods, Gulf Prairies

Stan's Notes: Sometimes planted as an ornamental tree. Does well in moist soils within the shade of larger trees. One of the last trees to produce leaves each spring, appearing dead until its flowers bud. The genus name *Chionanthus* is Latin for "snow flower" and refers to the flower color. Occasionally called Old Man's Beard because its thin flowers appear like the white hair of an elderly gentleman.

bark

flower

fruit

Southern Catalpa
Catalpa speciosa

SIMPLE OPPOSITE

Family: Trumpet-creeper (Bignoniaceae)

Height: 50–75' (15–23 m)

Tree: single trunk, large round crown

Leaf: simple, heart-shaped, 6–12" (15–30 cm) long, oppositely attached or whorls of 3 leaves, smooth edge (margin), dull green

Bark: light brown with deep furrows, flat-topped ridges

Flower: large and showy orchid-like flower, cream to white with yellow and purple spots and stripes, 2–3" (5–7.5 cm) long, in clusters, 5–8" (13–20 cm) wide, fragrant

Fruit: long bean-like green capsule, turning to brown at maturity, 8–18" (20–45 cm) long, splitting open into 2 parts, containing winged seeds

Fall Color: yellow green, turning black

Origin/Age: non-native; 40–50 years

Habitat: rich moist soils, sun

Range: planted in parks, yards and old home sites

Stan's Notes: Catalpa tree leaves are among the largest leaves in the state. Of about a dozen catalpa species, only two are native to North America. Successfully planted in landscapes in Texas. "Catalpa" is an American Indian name for this tree, but it is also called Catawba, Cigartree or Indianbean, which all refer to its large seedpods (fruit). Also known as Western Catalpa. Large showy flowers bloom during spring and attract many insects. Twigs have a soft white pith.

bark

flower

Saltcedar

Tamarix pentandra

Family: Tamarix (Tamaricaceae)

Height: 10–15' (3–4.6 m)

Tree: large shrub to small tree with a single or multiple trunks, both forms with slender arching branches, irregular spreading crown

Leaf: simple, lance-shaped, ¼–½" (.6–1 cm) long, alternately attached, sharply pointed tip, broadest near the base, scale-like, pale green, covered with a whitish waxy coating

Bark: reddish brown, smooth, turning rough with age

Flower: small pink-to-white flower, ¼" (.6 cm) diameter, in clusters on a stalk at the end of branch

Fruit: small green dry capsule, turning reddish brown at maturity, round, ½" (1 cm) wide, splitting open and releasing seeds

Fall Color: semi-evergreen

Origin/Age: non-native, introduced from Eurasia; 25–50 years

Habitat: wet soils, along streams, washes, rivers and other wet places, roadsides, sun

Range: scattered throughout Texas

Stan's Notes: Resembles junipers, but is not a conifer, lacking cones. An attractive tree along most rivers, washes and other wet places. There are several species, all similar; thus, much confusion occurs when identifying. All species are non-native and have spread across the Southwest. Capable of exuding excess salt from water, enabling it to tolerate a wide range of wetland habitats. Forms thick, impenetrable thickets that crowd out and out-compete native species for precious water resources. Eradication programs across the Southwest remove and replace this species with native trees and shrubs.

bark

fruit

Utah Serviceberry
Amelanchier utahensis

SIMPLE ALTERNATE

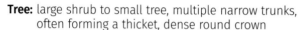

Family: Rose (Rosaceae)

Height: 10–25' (3–7.6 m)

Tree: large shrub to small tree, multiple narrow trunks, often forming a thicket, dense round crown

Leaf: simple, oval, ½–1½" (1–4 cm) long, alternately attached, blunt tip, toothed margin above the middle, leathery, yellowish green above and paler below, whitish hairs (sometimes smooth) on both surfaces, leafstalk ¼–½" (.6–1 cm) long, covered with tiny hairs or sometimes smooth

Bark: light reddish gray, thin and smooth, shallow cracks

Flower: 5–petaled white-to-pink flower, 1" (2.5 cm) wide, upright in clusters, 1–3" (2.5–7.5 cm) tall

Fruit: round green berry-like fruit (pome), becoming brown to dark purple to black at maturity, edible, ¼" (.6 cm) diameter, hanging in clusters on a fruit stalk, containing several small brown seeds

Fall Color: yellow to red

Origin/Age: native; 10–20 years

Habitat: well-drained soils between 7,000–7,500' (2,135–2,285 m), rocky slopes, canyons, sun

Range: Guadalupe Mountains in the Guadalupe National Park (western Texas), planted in parks and yards

Stan's Notes: One of several serviceberry species in North America. Scattered through the Rockies from Montana south to Arizona, New Mexico, California and Texas. Delicate white-to-pink flowers bloom before leaves in spring, turning into sweet fruit during fall. Birds and other wildlife enjoy the fruit. Deer browse twigs in winter. The wood is heavy and hard, but the tree is too small for commercial use.

bark

flower

fruit

Brasil
Condalia hookeri

Family: Buckthorn (Rhamnaceae)

Height: 20–30' (6.1–9.1 m)

Tree: small tree, single to many short trunks dividing close to the ground, branching in all directions, resulting in a broad irregular crown

Leaf: simple, spoon-shaped, 1–2" (2.5–5 cm) long, alternately attached, widest at the end, with a round or pointed tip, smooth edge (margin), smooth and shiny bright green above, paler and hairy below

Bark: gray to reddish brown, thin and smooth, becoming scaly with age

Flower: tiny green flower, ⅛" (.4 cm) wide, with no petals, stalkless, 1–3 flowers sprouting from the leaf base

Fruit: green berry (drupe), turning shiny black when mature, sweet and edible, ¼" (.6 cm) wide, with 1 flattened seed

Fall Color: semi-evergreen

Origin/Age: native; 75–100 years

Habitat: sandy soils, scrub, thickets, sun

Range: southern third of Texas excluding the Trans-Pecos, planted in parks and yards

Stan's Notes: Evergreen in southern Texas. Uncommon in northern Texas, where it turns yellow in fall before dropping its leaves. Often grows in dense thickets. Difficult to bushwhack through due to its thorn-like branches. Flowers any time in southern Texas. Produces many shiny, juicy dark berries. The fruit makes good jelly, and is eaten by a variety of wildlife. Also called Bluewood, referring to a dye extracted from the fruit and wood. Also called Purple Haw, Capul Negro or Logwood. Wood is heavy, hard and used for firewood.

bark

flower

fruit

Texas Madrone
Arbutus texana

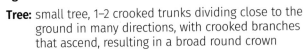

Family: Heath (Ericaceae)

Height: 20–30' (6.1–9.1 m)

Tree: small tree, 1–2 crooked trunks dividing close to the ground in many directions, with crooked branches that ascend, resulting in a broad round crown

Leaf: simple, oval, 1–3" (2.5–7.5 cm) long, alternately attached, with a blunt tip, smooth or fine-toothed margin, shiny and dark green above, paler below

Bark: reddish brown, thin, papery, peeling away in large scales, becoming deeply furrowed and darker with age, underlying bark smooth and white to orange

Flower: vase-shaped white-to-pink flower, ⅜" (.9 cm) long, in clusters on stout hairy stalks at ends of branches

Fruit: green pod, turning dark red when mature, with a granular or bumpy surface, ¼" (.6 cm) long

Fall Color: evergreen

Origin/Age: native; 200–250 years

Habitat: dry rocky soils, sandy soils, mountains, canyons, sun

Range: scattered in central and western Texas, planted in yards

Stan's Notes: A tree of the mountains of Texas, covered with pretty urn-shaped flowers in spring and red fruit in fall. Most known for its attractive exfoliating bark. When older layers of bark peel away, the underlying bark is smooth and color ranges from white to orange. Some have tan-to-red bark, which has led to other common names such as Lady's Legs. Also known as Manzanita ("little apple"), referring to the fruit. Many bird species eat the fruit, which helps spread the range of the tree when viable seeds are dropped.

bark

flower

fruit

Anacua
Ehretia anacua

Family: Borage (Boraginaceae)

Height: 20–40' (6.1–12.2 m)

Tree: single trunk or many trunks dividing close to the ground in many directions, ascending branches result in a broad round crown

Leaf: simple, oval, 1–3" (2.5–7.5 cm) long, alternately attached, widest at the middle, with a round or pointed tip, smooth margin or fine teeth, rough and dark green above, paler and hairy below

Bark: gray to reddish brown and thick, becoming scaly with age

Flower: 5–petaled, bell-shaped white flower, ⅜" (.9 cm) long, in large clusters, 1–3" (2.5–7.5 cm) long

Fruit: green fruit, turning yellow or orange at maturity, ¼" (.6 cm) wide, containing 2 seeds

Fall Color: semi-evergreen

Origin/Age: native; 75–100 years

Habitat: poor soils, sandy soils with good drainage, prairies, coastal flats, sun

Range: coastal and central Texas, planted in parks, yards

Stan's Notes: This is a small tree to large shrub that grows in poor soils. A popular ornamental tree, producing large flower clusters in March and April, making it attractive in landscapes. Evergreen in southern Texas, it drops its leaves in central Texas and farther north. Fruit ripens at summer's end and is eaten by many bird species and other wildlife. Since the tree never reaches a large size, the wood is used only for tool handles and fence posts. Common and species name is from *Anachuite*, the Spanish name for a similar tree. Also called Sandpapertree, Sugarberry, Knockaway and Manzanita.

flower

bark

fruit

thorn

Russian Olive

Elaeagnus angustifolia

Family: Oleaster (Elaeagnaceae)

Height: 10–20' (3–6.1 m)

Tree: single crooked trunk is often divided low, open irregular crown

Leaf: simple, lance-shaped, 1–4" (2.5–10 cm) long, alternately attached, blunt tip or sharp tip, margin lacking teeth, gray, leaves and twigs covered with grayish white hairs

Bark: light gray with shallow furrows, thorns on twigs

Flower: 4–petaled yellow flower, ¼–½" (.6–1 cm) wide

Fruit: gray-to-yellow olive-like dry fruit (drupe), ¼–½" (.6–1 cm) wide, containing 1 seed

Fall Color: brown

Origin/Age: non-native, introduced from Europe; 50–75 years

Habitat: wide variety of soils, sun to partial shade

Range: usually seen near old farmsteads, parks, formerly planted as an ornamental

Stan's Notes: This tree is usually seen in low to medium elevations, growing with cottonwood trees. Was planted in North America for its unusual gray leaves and olive-like fruit, often as a shelterbelt. While it is no longer planted, it has escaped from gardens, yards and parks and now grows in the wild (naturalized). Spread by birds, which pass the seeds through their digestive tracts unharmed. Twigs are often scaly and armed with very long thorns that have a salmon-colored pith. The species name *angustifolia* means "narrow leaf." Also called Oleaster or Narrow-leaved Oleaster.

fruit

bark

flower

Crab Apple
Malus spp.

Family: Rose (Rosaceae)

Height: 10–20' (3–6.1 m)

Tree: single crooked trunk, broad open crown

Leaf: simple, oval, 2–3" (5–7.5 cm) long, alternately attached, sometimes with shallow lobes, double-toothed margin, dark green above, lighter colored and usually smooth or hairless below

Bark: gray, many scales, with 1–2" (2.5–5 cm) long stout thorns often on twigs

Flower: 5–petaled white-to-pink or red flower that is often very showy, 1–2" (2.5–5 cm) wide

Fruit: apple (pome), ranging in color from green and yellow to red, edible, 1–3" (2.5–7.5 cm) diameter, single or in small clusters, hanging from a long fruit stalk well into winter

Fall Color: yellow to red

Origin/Age: native and non-native; 25–50 years

Habitat: wide variety of soils at low elevations, sun

Range: scattered throughout Texas, often around cities or old home sites, planted in yards

Stan's Notes: Many species of cultivated Crab Apple can be found throughout Texas. Others have escaped cultivation and now grow in the wild. Introduced to the United States in colonial times. Has since bred with native species, producing hybrids that are hard to identify. Now found throughout the country. Apples are closely related to those sold in grocery stores and have been used in jams and jellies. Cider is often made from the more tart apples. Fruit is an important food source for wildlife. Twigs often have long stout thorns, which are actually modified branches known as spur branches.

bark

fruit

River Birch
Betula nigra

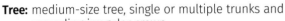

Family: Birch (Betulaceae)

Height: 40–60' (12.2–18 m)

Tree: medium-size tree, single or multiple trunks and spreading irregular crown

Leaf: simple, oval, 2–3" (5–7.5 cm) long, alternately attached, sometimes with asymmetrical leaf base, double-toothed margin, dark green above, paler green below

Bark: reddish brown to salmon pink, some shaggy curly bark, often flaky, becoming dark silver gray and scaly with age

Fruit: many winged nutlets, each ⅛" (.3 cm) wide, in a cone-like seed catkin, 1" (2.5 cm) long

Fall Color: yellow

Origin/Age: native; 50–75 years

Habitat: wet soils, in river valleys, along streams, wetlands and lakes, shade tolerant

Range: eastern edge of Texas, planted in parks and yards

Stan's Notes: This is the southernmost birch tree species in North America, growing as far south as Texas and Florida, and the only birch to disperse its seeds in spring. "River" refers to its habitat near water, where it plays a major role in erosion control. "Birch" comes from the Old German birka, meaning "bright," presumably referring to its light bark. Trunk can grow to 12–18 inches (30–45 cm) wide and is often covered with a salmon pink curled bark. Widely planted as a landscape tree. It is the only native birch resistant to Bronze Birch Borer beetle larvae, which tunnel through the inner bark, causing branches or the entire tree to die. The wood is rarely used for any commercial application.

bark

flower

fruit

Southern Wax-myrtle
Myrica cerifera

Family: Bayberry (Myricaceae)

Height: 15–30' (4.6–9.1 m)

Tree: small tree, often appearing like a large shrub, multiple small trunks, broad round crown

Leaf: simple, lance-shaped, 1–5" (2.5–13 cm) long, alternately attached, with a coarse-toothed margin beyond the middle; thick, aromatic, shiny yellowish green or grayish green above, paler with yellow dots below

Bark: light gray, thin and smooth

Flower: small red flower, ½" (1 cm) long, in compact oval clusters located at the leaf base

Fruit: warty green berry (drupe), covered with bluish wax when mature, round, ⅛" (.3 cm) wide, in clusters, containing 1 seed

Fall Color: semi-evergreen

Origin/Age: native; 50–100 years

Habitat: sandy soils, swamps, pinelands, sun to shade

Range: eastern quarter of Texas

Stan's Notes: Clusters of bluish berries make this tree an attractive ornamental to plant in yards. Planted around homes for its aromatic oil in the leaves, which reportedly repels insects. Can be pruned to appear like a shrub. Fruit attracts much wildlife. A hardy tree that can tolerate a wide range of growing conditions such as high salt concentrations in the soil. Usually evergreen, but will drop its leaves in winter if it gets too cold (semi-evergreen). A sprig of leaves placed in a drawer or closet is supposed to keep insect pests away. Many settlers used the wax from the berries to make candles. Also called Bayberry, Candleberry or Tallow Shrub.

flower

bark

fruit

Leatherwood
Cyrilla racemiflora

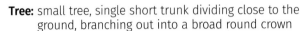

Family: Cyrilla (Cyrillaceae)

Height: 10–20' (3–6.1 m)

Tree: small tree, single short trunk dividing close to the ground, branching out into a broad round crown

Leaf: simple, lance-shaped, 2–4" (5–10 cm) long, alternately attached, widest at the middle, with a round or slightly pointed tip, leathery, smooth edge, smooth and bright green above, paler below

Bark: gray to reddish brown, thin and smooth

Flower: 5–petaled white-to-reddish flower, ⅛" (.4 cm) wide, many flowers in long narrow clusters at the ends of small branches

Fruit: green fruit, ⅛" (.3 cm) wide, turning brown and papery at maturity

Fall Color: semi-evergreen

Origin/Age: native; 75–100 years

Habitat: moist soils, wet soils, river valleys, along streams, wetlands, sun

Range: far eastern edge of Texas excluding the Gulf coast, planted in parks and yards

Stan's Notes: A small, native semi-evergreen tree found growing in moist to wet areas of extreme eastern Texas. It ranges from the East coast down throughout Florida and west to Texas. The genus *Cyrilla* includes only this species in the southeastern United States. Usually it grows like a shrub along flowing streams and clear rivers. Often associated with pine trees. Leaves often remain on the tree until the following summer before being replaced with new ones. Planted in landscapes including parks and yards.

thorn

bark

flower

fruit

Hawthorn
Crataegus spp.

SIMPLE
ALTERNATE

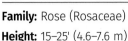

Family: Rose (Rosaceae)

Height: 15–25' (4.6–7.6 m)

Tree: short round tree, single trunk, round crown

Leaf: simple, oval to triangular, 2–4" (5–10 cm) long, alternately attached, some have 3 lobes, double-toothed margin, thick, shiny dark green

Bark: gray with red patches, very scaly and covered with peeling bark, sturdy thorns, 1–3" (2.5–7.5 cm) long

Flower: 5–petaled white (occasionally pink) flower, 1–2" (2.5–5 cm) wide, in flat-topped clusters, 3–5" (7.5–13 cm) wide, fragrant

Fruit: red or orange apple-like fruit (pome), often called haws, edible, ½–1" (1–2.5 cm) wide, in clusters

Fall Color: red to orange

Origin/Age: native and non-native; 50–100 years

Habitat: dry soils, canyons, prairies, hillsides, full sun

Range: mostly in the eastern half of Texas, 1–2 species in western Texas, planted in yards and parks

Stan's Notes: Over 100 hawthorn species in North America, at least 13 native to Texas and more than 1,100 hybrids in the United States. Species in Texas include Downy Hawthorn (the widest distribution), Cockspur Hawthorn (one of the most common), Littlehip Hawthorn (the most numerous in eastern Texas), Pear Hawthorn (in far eastern Texas in only 2–3 counties), Gregg Hawthorn (the rarest), Blueberry Hawthorn (the largest), Barberry Hawthorn, Reverchon Hawthorn, Mayhaw, Texas Hawthorn, Tracy Hawthorn, Parsley Hawthorn and Green Hawthorn. Birds nest in the tree for some thorny protection. Butcher Birds (shrikes) will impale prey on branch and trunk thorns. Indigenous peoples used the thorns for tools requiring a long point.

fruit

bark

flower

Carolina Buckthorn
Rhamnus caroliniana

Family: Buckthorn (Rhamnaceae)

Height: 15–40' (4.6–12.2 m)

Tree: small tree to large shrub, single straight branching or multiple crooked trunks, round crown

Leaf: simple, oval, 2–4½" (5–11 cm) long, alternately attached, widest at the middle, with a pointed tip, few teeth, covered with dark hairs when young, dark green with hairs below when mature

Bark: light gray and smooth, slightly furrowed with age

Flower: bell-shaped green-to-yellow flower, ¼" (.6 cm) long, in small clusters

Fruit: green berry, turning black at maturity, edible, ¼" (.6 cm) wide, in clusters, containing 2–4 seeds and remaining on the tree throughout winter

Fall Color: yellow

Origin/Age: native; 25–50 years

Habitat: wide variety of soils, moist river bottoms, along streams, understories, sun to shade

Range: eastern half of Texas excluding the southern tip

Stan's Notes: About 100 buckthorn tree and shrub species, with 12 native to North America and 1–2 European species that escaped from landscaping and are now found in the wild. Ranges from Florida and Georgia west to central Texas. In Texas it often grows only to 15 feet (4.6 m), but can grow to 40 feet (12.2 m). Slow growing, short lived, often appearing more like a shrub. Flowers in May, with edible fruit maturing in September and October. Many bird species feed on the berries. Deer and other large mammals browse the leaves and twigs. Despite being a buckthorn, it has no thorns. First seen and described in South Carolina, hence the common and species names.

bark

fruit

American Hornbeam

Carpinus caroliniana

SIMPLE ALTERNATE

Family: Birch (Betulaceae)

Height: 15–25' (4.6–7.6 m)

Tree: single to multiple crooked trunks, wide and often flat crown

Leaf: simple, oval, 2–5" (5–13 cm) long, alternately attached, with a pointed tip and asymmetrical leaf base, sharp double-toothed margin, light green

Bark: light blue-gray to gray, very smooth and unbroken with longitudinal muscle-like ridges

Fruit: many small ribbed nutlets, each ¼" (.6 cm) wide, contained in a leaf-like papery green bract, 2–4" (5–10 cm) long, that hangs in clusters and turns brown when mature

Fall Color: orange to deep red

Origin/Age: native; 50–75 years

Habitat: rich moist soils, moist valleys, along streams and other wet places, partial shade

Range: eastern edge of Texas

Stan's Notes: This is mostly an understory tree in the Pineywoods and Gulf Prairies and Marshes. One of about 25 species in *Carpinus*, the American Hornbeam is the only one native to North America. An easily recognized species, with its smooth unbroken trunk and long, fluted muscle-like ridges. Also known as Musclewood, Blue Beech, Water Beech and Ironwood. "Horn" in the common name means "tough" and "beam" means "tree" in Old English, describing its tough wood. The wood is used for tool handles.

bark

fruit

American Beech
Fagus grandifolia

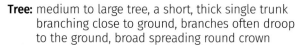

Family: Beech (Fagaceae)

Height: 60–80' (18–24 m)

Tree: medium to large tree, a short, thick single trunk branching close to ground, branches often droop to the ground, broad spreading round crown

Leaf: simple, oval, 2–5" (5–13 cm) long, alternately attached, long pointed tip, straight parallel veins, each ends in a sharp shallow tooth, leathery dark green above, lighter green below

Bark: light gray, smooth

Fruit: reddish brown capsule, ½–1½" (1–4 cm) long, in pairs, splitting open into 4 sections to release a 3–sided nut

Fall Color: yellow to brown

Origin/Age: native; 150–200 years

Habitat: well-drained moist soils, bottomlands, deciduous forests, shade tolerant

Range: eastern edge of Texas in the Pineywoods, planted in parks and around homes

Stan's Notes: Highly prized tree with important benefits to wildlife. Squirrels, grouse, bears, raccoons, deer and many other animals eat the abundant and edible beechnuts. Unusual bark in that it remains smooth even as the tree matures. The wood is very valuable and has been used for many years in furniture and flooring. One of the most abundant, well-recognized trees in eastern North America. Grows in mixed deciduous forests with oaks and maples. Can grow in pure stands. Has been planted in parks and around homes for many years. Until a larger tree falls, allowing enough light and room to grow, young saplings can sustain in dense shade for years.

bark

flower

fruit

SIMPLE
ALTERNATE

Two-winged Silverbell
Halesia diptera

Family: Storax (Styracaceae)

Height: 20–30' (6.1–9.1 m)

Tree: small tree or large shrub, single or multiple straight trunks, open crown

Leaf: simple, oval, 2–5" (5–13 cm) long, alternately attached, widest at the middle, irregular fine teeth, hairy when young, becoming smooth with age, dark green above, paler below

Bark: brown to reddish brown, furrowed with many long, narrow scaly ridges

Flower: 4–petaled, bell-shaped white flower, ½–1" (1–2.5 cm) long, hanging in clusters of 2–5 on a long stalk

Fruit: 2–winged green pod-like fruit (drupe), becoming brown and papery when mature, 1–2" (2.5–5 cm) long, hanging in clusters, containing 2–3 seeds

Fall Color: yellow

Origin/Age: native; 50–100 years

Habitat: moist to wet soils, along streams, wetlands, partial shade to sun

Range: eastern edge of Texas, southern Pineywoods, planted in parks and yards

Stan's Notes: This tree is seen from Georgia to northern Florida to eastern Texas. Once established, not much water is needed. A pest-free and disease-free tree with attractive flowers blooming in March and April, making it desirable for gardens. Bees attracted to the flowers produce a flavorful honey. Squirrels and other small animals eat the fruit in fall. Wood has been used for cabinetry and carving. Also called Snowdroptree, Snowbell or just Silverbell.

bark

flower

fruit

American Smoketree
Cotinus obovatus

Family: Sumac or Cashew (Anacardiaceae)

Height: 20–30' (6.1–9.1 m)

Tree: small tree with a single short straight trunk, wide spreading branches, open round crown

Leaf: simple, ovate, 2–6" (5–15 cm) long, alternately attached, widest at the middle or base, with a rounded or notched tip, wavy edge, dull green above, slightly paler below with a few silky hairs

Bark: gray to dark brown and thin, scaly with age

Flower: 5–petaled white-to-pink flower, ¼" (.6 cm) wide, in large upright clusters, 4–6" (10–15 cm) tall

Fruit: green flat dry fruit (drupe), turning pale brown when mature, ⅛" (.3 cm) diameter, in clusters, remaining on the tree in winter, containing 1 seed

Fall Color: orange to red

Origin/Age: native; 100–200 years

Habitat: dry rocky soils, sandy soils, limestone soils, hillsides, along roads, scrublands, forest edges, sun

Range: isolated in a small pocket in central Texas, in Kerr, Kendall, Bandera and Uvalde Counties

Stan's Notes: An unimpressive tree found in the hard limestone soil of a few central Texas counties. Some think the population is a relic from 25 million years ago, isolated from a former range that reached across northeastern Texas into Oklahoma, Arkansas and Tennessee. Not found anywhere in great abundance anymore. Flowers cover the tree early in spring, appearing like pink smoke from a distance, hence its common name. Some say the fruit looks like smoke from a distance during winter. Wood has been used to make a yellow dye. Not the same tree at nurseries, which is a hybrid from Eurasia.

flower

bark

fruit

Sweetleaf
Symplocos tinctoria

Family: Sweetleaf (Symplocaceae)

Height: 20–35' (6.1–10.7 m)

Tree: small tree with a single short crooked trunk, wide spreading branches and open irregular crown

Leaf: simple, lance-shaped, 2–6" (5–15 cm) long, alternately attached, 1–2½" (2.5–6 cm) wide, widest at the middle, pointed at the tip and base, smooth edge or sometimes with few teeth, shiny and dark green above, paler below with yellowish hairs

Bark: gray to reddish brown, thin and smooth, becoming warty with age

Flower: 5–petaled white-to-yellow flower, ⅜" (.9 cm) wide, with petals fusing at the base to form a tube (corolla), in clusters along the ends of branches where the leaves attach

Fruit: egg-shaped green berry-like fruit (drupe), turning pale brown at maturity, ½" (1 cm) long, with 1 seed

Fall Color: evergreen

Origin/Age: native; 100–200 years

Habitat: sandy soils, pine forests, along roads, scrublands, forest edges, partial shade to sun

Range: isolated in a small pocket in far eastern and northeastern Texas, Pineywoods

Stan's Notes: An uncommon tree, covered with attractive flowers from February to April and laden with brown fruit in late summer. Common name refers to its tasty leaves, which wildlife and livestock eat. Because horses browse the leaves, also called Horsesugar. Species *tinctoria* refers to a yellow dye that was once obtained from the twigs and leaves. Ranges from Virginia to Florida and west to Texas.

bark

flower

fruit

Texas Redbud
Cercis canadensis texensis

Family: Pea or Bean (Fabaceae)

Height: 15–25' (4.6–7.6 m)

Tree: small tree, single or multiple thin trunks with low branching, horizontal branching on an umbrella-like spreading crown

Leaf: simple, heart-shaped, 2–6" (5–15 cm) long, alternately attached, pointed tip, smooth margin, shiny dark green, leafstalk swollen at the top

Bark: gray, smooth with reddish streaks, becoming scaly with age

Flower: pea-like lavender-to-pink flower, ¼" (.6 cm) wide, along the branches

Fruit: reddish brown pod, 2–4" (5–10 cm) long, pointed at both ends, on a short fruit stalk

Fall Color: yellow

Origin/Age: native; 50–75 years

Habitat: moist soils, along streams, forest edges, shade

Range: eastern quarter of Texas, planted in parks, gardens

Stan's Notes: An understory tree that is tolerant of shade. In many places it would not be spring without the spectacular display of its purplish pink flowers, which bloom before the leaves appear. Also known as American Redbud or Judastree, the latter name referring to a legend that this was the species Judas used to hang himself, and that the once white flowers are now forever red with shame. One of two *Cercis* species native to North America. The second species is seen in Arizona, California and Nevada. Texas Redbud is a nearly identical variety, or subspecies, of Eastern Redbud (*C. canadensis*), which is found throughout the eastern United States.

bark

flower

fruit

Redbay
Persea borbonia

Family: Laurel (Lauraceae)

Height: 40–60' (12.2–18 m)

Tree: medium-size tree, short trunk divided into multiple small trunks, dense round crown

Leaf: simple, lance-shaped, 2–6" (5–15 cm) long, alternately attached, thick, bright green above, paler with white hairs below, aromatic

Bark: dark red to brown, thin when young, becoming furrowed with age

Flower: light yellow flower, ⅓" (.8 cm) wide, on a short stalk, ½–1" (1–2.5 cm) long, in small clusters

Fruit: green berry (drupe), turning shiny black when mature, round, ½" (1 cm) wide, on a fruit stalk, ½–1" (1–2.5 cm) long, containing many seeds

Fall Color: evergreen

Origin/Age: native; 50–100 years

Habitat: moist to wet soils, along streams and swamps, partial shade to full sun

Range: southeastern Texas, Pineywoods, Gulf Prairies, planted in parks and yards

Stan's Notes: A member of the Laurel family and closely related to Sassafras (pg. 255). Its aromatic leaves are used to flavor soups and meats. The leaves have been used as a substitute for bay leaves, a common spice that usually comes from the Bay Laurel (not shown), a European species in the same family. Squirrels and birds eat the fruit, which is bitter. Wood has been used in boat construction and furniture. Planted along streets and parking lots and in other urban areas because of its ability to tolerate a variety of growing conditions.

thorn

bark

flower

fruit

Osage-orange
Maclura pomifera

Family: Mulberry (Moraceae)

Height: 30–40' (9.1–12.2 m)

Tree: small to medium tree with a short, often crooked trunk, many spreading branches, irregular crown

Leaf: simple, oval, 3–5" (7.5–13 cm) long, alternately attached, long pointed tip, round to heart-shaped base, often wavy margin, no teeth, shiny dark green above, lighter below and lacking hairs, with thorns, 1" (2.5 cm) long, at the leaf base

Bark: gray to brown with narrow forking ridges, orange inner bark where bark has been removed

Flower: green-to-cream flower, in clusters, 1" (2.5 cm) wide, on a thin stalk, 2–3" (5–7.5 cm) long

Fruit: hard, grainy fleshy ball (pome), 3–5" (7.5–13 cm) wide, with a milky sap, many small brown seeds

Fall Color: yellow

Origin/Age: native; 100–200 years (some reach 350–400 years)

Habitat: deep rich soils and moist soils, river valleys, sun

Range: narrow band in eastern Texas along the Blackland Prairies, planted in parks and yards, along streets, as windbreaks and hedgerows

Stan's Notes: An ornamental tree named after the Osage Indians, who made bows and clubs from the wood, and its dimpled fruit, which has skin like an orange. Also known as Mock Orange, Horse Apple or Hedge Apple. Planted around homesteads before barbed wire was available, with thorns serving as fences. Wood is durable, but not used commercially. A yellow substance from the roots was used to dye clothing and baskets. This was the first tree sample Lewis and Clark sent back from the Louisiana Territory in 1804.

bark

flower

fruit

Carolina Basswood
Tilia caroliniana

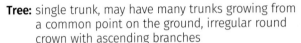

Family: Linden (Tiliaceae)

Height: 40–60' (12.2–18 m)

Tree: single trunk, may have many trunks growing from a common point on the ground, irregular round crown with ascending branches

Leaf: simple, heart-shaped, 3–7" (7.5–18 cm) long, alternately attached, with an asymmetrical leaf base, sharp-toothed margin, dark green above, lighter green below with light brown hairs

Bark: light gray color and smooth when young, darkens with long, narrow flat-topped ridges dividing into a short block with age, inner bark fibrous

Flower: creamy yellow flower, 1–2" (2.5–5 cm) wide, in clusters of 8–14 on a long stalk, 1–2" (2.5–5 cm) long, fragrant scent

Fruit: nut-like green fruit, turning yellow when mature, round, ¼" (.6 cm) diameter, covered with light brown hairs, on a 1–2" (2.5–5 cm) long fruit stalk, hanging in clusters from a leaf-like wing

Fall Color: yellow

Origin/Age: native; 100–150 years

Habitat: moist soils, river bottoms, creeks, shade to sun

Range: eastern quarter of Texas and a population in 7–8 central Texas counties, planted in parks and yards

Stan's Notes: Once found in many parts of Texas. When one tree dies, many suckering trees quickly sprout. Its smooth-grained soft wood is used for carving. Inner bark was used to make mats, rope and baskets. Once thought to be a subspecies of American Basswood (*T. americana*). Also called Basswood or American Linden.

bark

flower

fruit

Texas Olive
Cordia boissieri

Family: Borage (Boraginaceae)

Height: 20–30' (6.1–9.1 m)

Tree: small tree with a straight trunk, full round crown

Leaf: simple, oval, 4–6" (10–15 cm) long, widest at the middle, alternately attached, with a pointed tip, wavy edge with a few round teeth, slightly rough to touch and dark green above, paler below

Bark: gray to light brown, thick, many thin flat-topped ridges

Flower: large white flower with a yellow center, 1–2" (2.5–5 cm) wide, in clusters at ends of small branches

Fruit: green fruit, turning bright reddish brown when mature, egg-shaped, 1" (2.5 cm) wide, in a papery cover (calyx), containing 1 seed

Fall Color: semi-evergreen

Origin/Age: native; 100–200 years

Habitat: dry rocky soils, sandy soils, along roads, scrublands, chaparral, forest edges, sun

Range: southern tier of Texas counties in the Rio Grande Valley, planted in parks and yards as far north as San Antonio

Stan's Notes: A wonderful native of southern Texas, but planted as far north as San Antonio. Usually evergreen, this tree drops its leaves and dies back in cold winters (semi-evergreen). Produces clusters of large, showy white flowers in spring. Will flower in any season if watered on a regular basis. Often planted in yards and parks due to its pretty blooms and colorful fruit, which ripens in fall. Does not produce olives, as the common name implies, but its fruit is eaten by wildlife of all kinds and livestock.

base bark

bark

fruit

cross section

Sycamore
Platanus occidentalis

Family: Sycamore (Platanaceae)

Height: 60–90' (18–27 m)

Tree: large tree, often a single massive trunk, enlarged at the base, open widely spreading crown

Leaf: simple, triangular, 4–8" (10–20 cm) long, alternately attached, 3–5 shallow pointed lobes, wavy coarse-toothed margin, 3 prominent veins, bright green above, paler below

Bark: pale white color, smooth, peeling off in large thin sections, green and cream-to-white inner bark produces a mottled effect, bark at the base of tree (see inset) often much darker than upper bark

Fruit: light brown round aggregate of many nutlets, 1" (2.5 cm) in diameter, hanging from a long fruit stalk, remaining on the tree into winter

Fall Color: brown

Origin/Age: native; 200–250 years

Habitat: moist soils, rich bottomlands, sun to partial shade

Range: eastern half of Texas except for the extreme south, planted in parks and yards

Stan's Notes: Produces a massive white trunk, larger in diameter than many other trees in Texas, which makes it easy to identify. Its branches are often crooked, making this species easy to climb. Some hollow trunks of large old trees are used by many animals and birds as homes. It is a fast-growing tree that usually grows in old fields or along streams. Often planted as an ornamental tree in landscapes or parks. Also called Buttonballtree, American Sycamore or American Planetree. Of the ten sycamore tree species, three are in the United States and one is in Canada.

bark

flower

fruit

Pawpaw
Asimina triloba

Family: Custard-apple (Annonaceae)

Height: 20–30' (6.1–9.1 m)

Tree: single or multiple straight trunks, straight branches, broad crown

Leaf: simple, obovate, 7–10" (18–25 cm) long, alternately attached, widest near the tip, smooth toothless margin, medium green above, paler below, on a short leafstalk (petiole)

Bark: brown, smooth, thin, covered with tiny bumps

Flower: triangular flower, 1–2" (2.5–5 cm) wide, made of 6 reddish purple petals, solitary or in small clusters nodding on the stalk, unpleasant odor

Fruit: green berry-like fruit (pome), turning yellow to brown or black at maturity, soft edible flesh with a prune-like texture and fruity custard flavor, round to slightly curved, 3–5" (7.5–13 cm) long, single or in small clusters, several large seeds, each ½" (1 cm) wide

Fall Color: yellow

Origin/Age: native; 100–150 years

Habitat: moist soils, floodplains, understories, shade

Range: far eastern edge of Texas, Pineywoods, planted in parks and yards

Stan's Notes: An unusual understory tree with large leaves and tiny banana-shaped fruit. Also called Wild Banana or Poor Man's Banana. A member of a mostly tropical tree family that produces fruit such as soursops and custard apples. New shoots grow from roots, forming large thickets or colonies. Flowers appear with leaves. Fruit, eaten by American Indians and early settlers, is sold in some stores today.

flower

Hairy Mountain-mahogany
Cercocarpus montanus paucidentatus

Family: Rose (Rosaceae)

Height: 5–15' (1.5–4.6 m)

Tree: very small tree, often shrub-like, multiple or single crooked trunks, dense round crown

Leaf: simple, wedge-shaped, ½–1" (1–2.5 cm) long, alternately attached, widest at the tip, large round teeth at tip, rolled margin, leathery, grayish green above, paler below

Bark: light reddish brown, thin and smooth, forming shallow fissures and scales with age

Flower: green-to-pink tubular flower, ¼" (.6 cm) long, with no petals, stalkless, 1–2 flowers sprouting from the base of leaf, pleasantly fragrant

Fruit: brown drupe-like dry fruit, cylindrical, ⅓" (.8 cm) long, tipped with an elongated hairy white plume up to 3" (7.5 cm) long

Fall Color: semi-evergreen

Origin/Age: native; 100–150 years

Habitat: dry gravelly soils above 5,000' (1,525 m), valleys, mountainsides, hillsides, sun

Range: isolated and scattered in western Texas

Stan's Notes: The Hairy Mountain-mahogany can be seen on slopes and mountainsides in Texas in Trans-Pecos region elevations above 5,000 feet (1,525 m). Range extends from Arizona east across New Mexico to western Texas, with a few scattered pockets in Mexico. This species has only slightly smaller leaves, flowers and fruit than the very similar Alderleaf Mountain-mahogany (pg. 139).

bark

fruit

Alderleaf Mountain-mahogany
Cercocarpus montanus

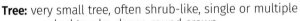

Family: Rose (Rosaceae)

Height: 5–15' (1.5–4.6 m)

Tree: very small tree, often shrub-like, single or multiple crooked trunks, dense round crown

Leaf: simple, wedge-shaped, ¾–1" (2–2.5 cm) long, alternately attached, widest at the tip, large round teeth at tip, grayish green above, paler with dense white hairs below, on a short leafstalk, ¼" (.6 cm) long

Bark: reddish brown, thick and rough when young, becoming deeply furrowed and scaly with age

Flower: green-to-pink tubular flower, ½" (1 cm) long, with no petals, stalkless, 1–3 flowers sprouting from the base of leaf, pleasantly fragrant

Fruit: brown drupe-like dry fruit, cylindrical, ½" (1 cm) long, covered with long hairs, tipped with an elongated hairy white plume up to 3" (7.5 cm) long

Fall Color: semi-evergreen

Origin/Age: native; 100–150 years

Habitat: dry gravelly soils, valleys, canyons, sun

Range: scattered in northern and western Texas

Stan's Notes: Mountain-mahogany trees in Texas appear similar and are hard to differentiate. Some group all into one species; others separate them into three. The flower tube, called a corolla, is divided at one end and looks like it has five petals. *Cercocarpus*, Greek for "tailed fruit," describes the long hairy plume on seeds. The bristle-like plume (awn) at the tip of the fruit body is much longer than the body. "Mahogany" refers to the richly colored hardwood. Also called True Mountain-mahogany or Silver Mountain-mahogany.

bark

flower

fruit

Yaupon
Ilex vomitoria

Family: Holly (Aquifoliaceae)

Height: 20–25' (6.1–7.6 m)

Tree: large shrub to small tree with many thin trunks branching near the ground, round crown

Leaf: simple, oval, ½–1½" (1–4 cm) long, alternately attached, widest at the middle, round (seldom pointed) tip, shallow round teeth, thick, smooth and leathery, shiny dark green above, paler below

Bark: light reddish brown, thin and smooth

Flower: 4–petaled single white flower with a green center, located at upper leaf junctions

Fruit: green berry-like fruit (drupe), turning dark red at maturity, ¼–⅓" (.6–.8 cm) wide, on a short fruit stalk, containing several grooved seeds (nutlets)

Fall Color: evergreen

Origin/Age: native; 50–100 years

Habitat: moist soils, wet soils, along streams and rivers, valleys, shade tolerant

Range: upper Texas coast, Pineywoods, eastern quarter of the state, planted in landscapes as an ornamental

Stan's Notes: Another holly species without "holly" in the common name. Seen mainly on the upper Texas coast, with solid thickets of it in many areas in southeastern Texas. Slow growing, often forming thickets along streams and slow-moving rivers. More like a shrub except when growing in very wet conditions. Reproduces by suckering genetically identical shoots and from seed. Flowers bloom in March and April. Fruit ripens in October to November. Birds eat the fruit; deer browse branches. Leaves were used to make a tea to induce vomiting, hence the species name. Can be pruned and shaped.

bark

flower

fruit

Possum Haw
Ilex decidua

Family: Holly (Aquifoliaceae)

Height: 20–25' (6.1–7.6 m)

Tree: shrub to small tree with many thin straight trunks branching near the ground, broad round crown

Leaf: simple, elliptical, 1½–4" (4–10 cm) long, alternately attached, widest at the middle, with a narrow base, shallow round-toothed margin, thick, smooth and leathery, green above, paler below

Bark: light brown, thin and smooth, becoming rough with age

Flower: tiny flower, ¼" (.6 cm) long, single or in pairs on a short stalk at the leaf junction

Fruit: green berry-like fruit (drupe), turning bright red or orange (sometimes yellow) when mature, ¼–⅓" (.6–.8 cm) wide, with several grooved seeds (nutlets)

Fall Color: evergreen

Origin/Age: native; 50–100 years

Habitat: moist soils, wet soils, along streams, floodplains, shade tolerant

Range: eastern half of Texas

Stan's Notes: The common name of this tree does not reflect that this is another of the holly species in Texas. It is the widest ranging of all hollies in the state, ranging all across southeastern states from Maryland and Florida, reaching its western edge in Texas. Usually appears more shrub-like, reaching tree size and shape only when in wet river bottoms. Fast growing and short lived, flowering in April and May, with fruit maturing in late summer and early fall. Many bird species eat the fruit, and deer browse the branches. Its bright red berries have been used for winter holiday decorations.

bark

fruit

American Holly
Ilex opaca

Family: Holly (Aquifoliaceae)

Height: 40–60' (12.2–18 m)

Tree: medium tree with a single straight trunk and long, narrow tapering crown

Leaf: simple, elliptical, 2–4" (5–10 cm) long, alternately attached, with spiny tips, coarse teeth, thick and leathery, green above, yellow green below

Bark: light gray, thin and smooth, sometimes with warty growths

Fruit: green berry-like fruit (drupe), turning bright red when mature, ¼–⅓" (.6–.8 cm) wide, on a short fruit stalk, containing 4 tiny nutlets

Fall Color: evergreen

Origin/Age: native; 50–100 years

Habitat: moist to moderately wet soils, floodplains, mixed deciduous forests, shade tolerant

Range: eastern quarter of Texas

Stan's Notes: About 300 species of *Ilex* worldwide, with about a dozen native to the eastern and southern United States. Of these, three species grow large enough to be considered trees. Male and female flowers are on separate trees (dioecious), with fruit produced only from female blossoms. Ripe fruit is red and only rarely orange, maturing in late summer and fall and remaining on the tree well into winter. Fruit is bitter, but eaten by a wide variety of birds and some mammals. Seen along hedgerows and highways, where birds have deposited the seeds unharmed. Cut branches with bright red berry-like fruit and attractive, spiny evergreen leaves are popular for holiday decorating.

bark

fruit

Sandpaper Oak
Quercus vaseyana

Family: Beech (Fagaceae)

Height: 15–20' (4.6–6.1 m)

Tree: single or multiple short trunks, appearing shrub-like most of the time, occasionally tree-like, with branches near the ground, broad round crown

Leaf: simple, oblong, ½–2" (1–5 cm) long, alternately attached, large curved pointed teeth, thick and leathery, covered with rough stiff hairs, shiny yellowish green above, paler below

Bark: gray and thin with patchy ridges and scales

Fruit: green acorn, turning brown at maturity, ovate, ½–1" (1–2.5 cm) long, solitary or in pairs on a short stalk or without a stalk, cap covering the upper half of nut, maturing in 1 season

Fall Color: semi-evergreen

Origin/Age: native; 250–350 years

Habitat: rocky and sandy soils, hills, canyons, sun

Range: isolated pockets of central and western Texas

Stan's Notes: A small native tree to large shrub isolated in small pockets from central Texas west to New Mexico and Mexico. Easily hybridizes with other oaks, making the resulting species difficult to identify. There are several varieties of *Q. pungens*, with only slight variations to the leaves and acorns. Sandpaper Oak leaves are rough to touch, hence its common name. Also called Pungent Oak, Shin Oak, Scrub Live Oak or Encino. Member of the white oak group, which has acorns that mature in one season. This tree and others in the white oak group are highly susceptible to oak wilt, especially in central and northern Texas.

bark

flower

fruit

Shrub Live Oak
Quercus turbinella

SIMPLE
ALTERNATE

Family: Beech (Fagaceae)

Height: 5–15' (1.5–4.6 m)

Tree: single or multiple short trunks, appearing shrub-like, branches near the ground, broad round crown

Leaf: simple, oval, 1–2" (2.5–5 cm) long, alternately attached, large pointed teeth, thick, stiff, leathery, yellowish green above and covered with a powdery coating (bloom), paler and finely hairy below

Bark: gray and thick with patchy ridges and scales

Flower: green catkin, ¼" (.6 cm) long, composed of many tiny flowers, ⅛" (.3 cm) wide

Fruit: green acorn, turning brown at maturity, ovate, 1" (2.5 cm) long, solitary or in pairs on a short stalk or without a stalk, cap covering the upper quarter of nut, maturing in 1 season

Fall Color: semi-evergreen

Origin/Age: native; 250–350 years

Habitat: rocky soils at 4,000–5,000' (1,220–1,525 m), hills, mountain slopes, sun

Range: the three mountain ranges in the Trans-Pecos

Stan's Notes: This small oak species is found in higher elevations in Texas, ranging through southwestern states from California to far western Texas. Highly drought resistant. Acorns mature early (June and July) in one season and are large and abundant enough to be an important source of food for wildlife. Also called Turbinella Oak, California Scrub Oak, Sonoran Scrub Oak and Scrub Oak. Best identified by its spiny-toothed stiff leaves, which are covered with a white powder. Will hybridize with Gambel Oak (pg. 271).

bark

fruit

SIMPLE ALTERNATE

Mexican Blue Oak
Quercus oblongifolia

Family: Beech (Fagaceae)

Height: 10–30' (3–9.1 m)

Tree: single or multiple short trunks, many spreading branches, broad flattened crown

Leaf: simple, 1–2" (2.5–5 cm) long, alternately attached, widest near the tip, smooth to wavy edge, usually a round tip but can be pointed, thick and leathery, blue-green and smooth above, paler below

Bark: gray and thick, appearing checkered with age

Fruit: green acorn, turning brown at maturity, edible, ovate, ½–¾" (1–2 cm) long, solitary or in pairs on a short stalk, sometimes stalkless, cap covering the upper quarter of nut, maturing in 1 season

Fall Color: evergreen

Origin/Age: native; 250–350 years

Habitat: rocky soils from 4,500–5,000' (1,370–1,525 m), open hillsides, slopes, grasslands, canyons, sun

Range: restricted to a few isolated mountain ranges in the southern Trans-Pecos region

Stan's Notes: First discovered in the early 1970s. A native oak, not very common and not in pure stands. Grows in small pockets, often clinging to canyon walls. In many areas it is small, never getting larger than a shrub. Can be identified by its bluish leaves. The species name *oblongifolia* means "long and oblong leaves," describing them well. Ranges across southeastern Arizona to far southwestern New Mexico and Texas, extending down into Mexico. Mostly associated with open oak woodlands near the Mexican border on hillsides and mountain slopes. Flowers in spring. Acorns mature in the same season. Wildlife eat the acorns, while Indigenous peoples used them as a food source.

bark

fruit

underside

Netleaf Oak
Quercus rugosa

Family: Beech (Fagaceae)

Height: 10–40' (3–12.2 m)

Tree: single or multiple short trunks, almost shrub-like with many spreading branches, flattened crown

Leaf: simple, 1–2½" (2.5–6 cm) long, alternately attached, pointed tip, wavy edge (margin) with many coarse teeth, thick and leathery, prominent net-like veins, dark green to gray green above, duller and smooth below, may have some hairs

Bark: light brown to dark brown and thin

Fruit: green acorn, turning brown at maturity, ovate, ½–1" (1–2.5 cm) long, solitary, in pairs or groups of 3 on a long stalk up to 2" (5 cm), cap covering the upper quarter to half of nut, maturing in 1 season

Fall Color: semi-evergreen

Origin/Age: native; 250–350 years

Habitat: rocky soils from 4,500–7,000' (1,370–2,135 m), mountain slopes, sun

Range: restricted to a few isolated mountain ranges in the southern Trans-Pecos region

Stan's Notes: A small to medium tree or large shrub. Not common in Texas or any other part of its range, extending from southeastern Arizona into extreme southwestern Texas and into the mountains of Mexico. The most likely place to see this rare tree is on the South Rim trail in the Chisos Mountains. Can be identified by the prominent net-like veins in leaves, most evident on the underside (see inset). Species *rugosa* refers to the leaves and means "having many wrinkles or creases." Depending on weather, leaves remain on the tree well into winter, dropping in spring as new leaves appear.

bark

lobed leaf

Lacey Oak
Quercus laceyi

Family: Beech (Fagaceae)

Height: 20–30' (6.1–9.1 m)

Tree: small tree, single trunk, sometimes with many thin trunks forming a shrub, open wide crown

Leaf: simple, oblong to oval, 1–3" (2.5–7.5 cm) long, alternately attached, sometimes with several round lobes (see inset), with a rounded tip, no teeth, thick, peach-colored when young, dusky bluish gray (smoky) above when older, pale below

Bark: gray, thin and smooth when young, becoming patchy with age

Fruit: green acorn, turning brown at maturity, oblong, ¾–1" (2–2.5 cm) long, on a short stalk, shallow cap covering the upper third of nut, frequently in clusters or pairs, maturing in 1 season

Fall Color: yellow to gold

Origin/Age: native; 200–250 years

Habitat: rocky limestone soils, sandy soils, prairies, rolling hills, pastures, riverbanks, sun

Range: Edwards Plateau, planted in landscapes

Stan's Notes: A small, often shrubby tree confined to the Edwards Plateau in Texas and parts of northern Mexico. Grows tallest when near water. Easily distinguished from other oaks by the smoky cast of its leaves when seen from afar. Unique due to its highly variable leaf shape, with most leaves lacking lobes and some with several large lobes. Extremely drought resistant, making it a great tree to plant in landscapes. Prefers rocky limestone soils. Member of the white oak group.

Mohr Oak
Quercus mohriana

Family: Beech (Fagaceae)

Height: 10–20' (3–6.1 m)

Tree: small tree, sometimes with a single trunk, other times with many thin trunks forming a shrub, open wide crown

Leaf: simple, lance-shaped, 1–3" (2.5–7.5 cm) long, alternately attached, rounded or pointed tip, smooth margin or with coarse teeth, shiny light green above, pale with light gray hairs below

Bark: gray, thin and smooth when young, becoming furrowed with age

Fruit: green acorn, turning brown when mature, nearly round, ½–¾" (1–2 cm) long, on a short stalk, with a shallow cap covering the upper half of nut, maturing in 1 season

Fall Color: evergreen

Origin/Age: native; 200–250 years

Habitat: sandy soils, prairies, old fields, pastures, rolling hills, sun

Range: western half of Texas including the panhandle

Stan's Notes: More of a shrub than a tree, growing mainly in open fields and prairies in limestone soils. Reproduces by new shoots that sprout from underground rhizomes. These often form a thicket of shrubby trees known as a motte. Does not grow very tall and can grow again from its roots after being burned or cut, having adapted to fire. Member of the white oak group. Shares a portion of its range with Gray Oak (pg. 161), but differs from the Gray by its shiny light green leaves and lack of hairs on the upper surface.

bark

fruit

Texas Live Oak
Quercus fusiformis

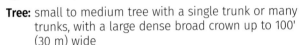

Family: Beech (Fagaceae)

Height: 30–40' (9.1–12.2 m)

Tree: small to medium tree with a single trunk or many trunks, with a large dense broad crown up to 100' (30 m) wide

Leaf: simple, oval, 1–3" (2.5–7.5 cm) long, alternately attached, pointed tip, smooth margin, no teeth, thick, dark green above, paler and with few hairs to densely hairy below

Bark: dark brown to reddish brown, thick with deep furrows, flat scales and ridges

Fruit: green acorn, turning brown when mature, edible, ¾" (2 cm) long, on a short stalk or no stalk, cap covering upper third of nut, maturing in 1 season

Fall Color: evergreen

Origin/Age: native; 150–250 years

Habitat: well-drained soils, prairies, sun

Range: central and coastal Texas

Stan's Notes: This is a smaller version of Live Oak (pg. 173), less common, but often confused with it. Where the two species occur together they produce hybrids, making them even more difficult to differentiate. Overall shorter in height and with smaller leaves than Live Oak, the Texas Live Oak will often form a thick multi-trunk shrub. Forms a large pure stand, called a motte, in the middle of a prairie. Reproduces by underground rhizomes that send up new genetically identical trees. Often these stands are dwarfs in size and shape. Highly susceptible to oak wilt. Occurs only in Texas and one area of southern Oklahoma. Also called West Texas Live Oak, Scrub Live Oak, Plateau Live Oak or just Live Oak.

bark

flower

fruit

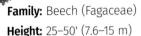

Gray Oak
Quercus grisea

Family: Beech (Fagaceae)

Height: 25–50' (7.6–15 m)

Tree: single or multiple short trunks, branching close to the ground, spreading round crown

Leaf: simple, 1–3" (2.5–7.5 cm) long, alternately attached, widest near the middle, single pointed tip, smooth edge, occasionally with 1–2 large teeth, thick and leathery, gray green with many fine hairs

Bark: dark gray and thick, with deep furrows with age

Flower: green-to-yellow catkin, 1" (2.5 cm) long, made up of many tiny flowers

Fruit: green acorn, turning brown at maturity, ovate, ¼–¾" (.6–2 cm) long, solitary or in pairs, growing on twigs of current year, stalkless, cap covers upper third of nut and covered with reddish brown hairs

Fall Color: evergreen

Origin/Age: native; 250–350 years

Habitat: rocky soils, canyons, sun

Range: western Texas, Trans-Pecos region only

Stan's Notes: Can be a large shrub in open dry areas. A medium tree growing in protected canyons in higher moisture soils, with the largest Gray Oak in Texas measuring 50 feet (15 m) tall. Range is across eastern Arizona into parts of New Mexico, western Texas and extends down into Mexico. Livestock and wild mammals browse the leaves and acorns. The leaves appear gray due to hairs covering both upper and lower surfaces. Hybridizes with other oak species, which sometimes makes this one hard to identify. Wood is of little commercial value, but it has been used for fence posts and firewood. Best value of this tree is for wildlife cover and food.

bark

flower

fruit

Emory Oak
Quercus emoryi

Family: Beech (Fagaceae)

Height: 25–50' (7.6–15 m)

Tree: single or multiple short trunks, branching close to the ground, spreading round crown

Leaf: simple, 1–3½" (2.5–9 cm) long, alternately attached, widest near the base, several large coarse teeth, thick, leathery and stiff, dark green and shiny above, duller below with hairs on young leaves, older leaves smooth

Bark: dark brown to nearly black, thick with deep fissures separated by broad thick plates with age

Flower: green-to-yellow hairy catkin, 1–2" (2.5–5 cm) long, composed of many tiny flowers, ⅛" (.3 cm) wide

Fruit: green acorn, turning brown at maturity, edible, ovate, ¼–¾" (.6–2 cm) long, solitary or in pairs, no stalk or on a short stalk, cap covering the upper third of nut, maturing in 1 season

Fall Color: evergreen

Origin/Age: native; 250–350 years

Habitat: moist soils at elevations above 4,500' (1,370 m), canyons, foothills, mountain slopes, sun

Range: southern Trans-Pecos region in the Chisos, Davis, Chinati and Vieja Mountains

Stan's Notes: Fairly uncommon in Texas, often only 25 feet (7.6 m) tall. Member of the black oak group, which usually has bitter acorns that take two years to mature. Emory acorns are not bitter, however, and mature in just one season. Acorns are low in tannin, making them palatable. Wood is heavy and strong, used for fence posts and firewood. Also called Black Oak, Blackjack Oak or Bellota.

bark

flower

fruit

Arizona White Oak
Quercus arizonica

Family: Beech (Fagaceae)

Height: 25–50' (7.6–15 m)

Tree: single or multiple short trunks, branching close to the ground, spreading round crown

Leaf: simple, 1–4" (2.5–10 cm) long, alternately attached, often widest near the middle, margin lacking teeth, leathery and stiff, dull bluish green above, duller and paler below with some hairs

Bark: light gray, thin and smooth when young, becoming rough and broken into furrows with age

Flower: green-to-yellow catkin, 1–3" (2.5–7.5 cm) long, composed of many tiny flowers, ⅛" (.3 cm) wide

Fruit: green acorn, turning brown at maturity, ovate, ¼–¾" (.6–2 cm) long, solitary on a long stalk, cap covering upper third of nut, maturing in 1 season

Fall Color: semi-evergreen

Origin/Age: native; 150–250 years

Habitat: rocky soils above 4,500' (1,370 m), canyons, hillsides, sun

Range: scattered and isolated in several mountain ranges in the Trans-Pecos region

Stan's Notes: An uncommon oak in Texas. Hybridizes with other oaks, making it hard to find a pure species. Nearly evergreen leaves allow the tree to remain green even in winter. New leaves emerge as old ones drop in May or June. Slow-growing. Flowers in spring and produces acorns in summer. Heavy acorn crop every couple years. Wildlife depend on nuts for food, but they are bitter and not highly prized. Dark wood is close-grained, very heavy and strong, which makes it hard to split for firewood but good for tool handles.

bark

Coast Laurel Oak
Quercus hemisphaerica

SIMPLE
ALTERNATE

Family: Beech (Fagaceae)

Height: 15–30' (4.6–9.1 m)

Tree: small tree with a single straight trunk or a clump forming a shrubby tree, dense broad round crown

Leaf: simple, narrow lance-shaped, 2–4" (5–10 cm) long, ½–1" (1–2.5 cm) diameter, alternately attached, pointed tip, slightly toothed wavy edge (margin), shiny bright green above, pale and smooth below

Bark: gray, thick and smooth when young, becoming deeply furrowed with narrow flat ridges with age

Fruit: green acorn, turning brown when mature, bitter, nearly round, ½–¾" (1–2 cm) long, on a short stalk, shallow scaly cap covering the upper quarter of nut, maturing in 2 seasons

Fall Color: semi-evergreen

Origin/Age: native; 25–50 years

Habitat: sandy soils, coastal prairies, sand dunes, sun

Range: coastal Texas, planted in parks and yards

Stan's Notes: So closely related to Laurel Oak (pg. 175), most do not consider it a different species. Others think it is another species, with a range from the Carolinas to Florida and west to Texas. Very fast growing and short lived, some consider it a weedy type of plant when compared with the other oak trees. Its many small acorns are eaten by a wide variety of birds and animals, which helps spread the range of the tree. The species name *hemisphaerica* refers to the hemispherical shape of the crown. Bred for use in the nursery trade and is planted in parks, yards and along streets in many regions. In other parts of the country the tree reaches 100 feet (30 m) tall. Also called Darlington Oak or Laurel Oak.

167

bark

fruit

Willow Oak
Quercus phellos

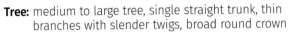

Family: Beech (Fagaceae)

Height: 50–80' (15–24 m)

Tree: medium to large tree, single straight trunk, thin branches with slender twigs, broad round crown

Leaf: simple, lance-shaped, 2–4" (5–10 cm) long and 1" (2.5 cm) wide, alternately attached, single tiny pointed tip (bristle-tipped), smooth (sometimes wavy) margin, light green, sometimes with tiny gray hairs on the underside

Bark: dark gray, smooth and hard, becoming nearly black with narrow ridges with age

Fruit: green acorn, turning brown when mature, edible, nearly round, ½" (1 cm) long, on a short stalk, shallow cap covering upper third of nut, maturing in 2 seasons

Fall Color: yellow

Origin/Age: native; 150–200 years

Habitat: moist soils, floodplains, river valleys and other lowlands, sun to partial shade

Range: eastern quarter of Texas in the Pineywoods and Gulf Prairies

Stan's Notes: This is a different-looking oak, with thin willow-like leaves and twigs. Can grow upwards of 100 feet (30 m), but usually reaches only around 50 feet (15 m). Able to survive with its roots covered for extended periods of time with standing water. Tolerant of heat, drought and air pollution. All sorts of wildlife eat the small acorns. A member of the black (also known as red) oak group, with acorns maturing in two seasons. Also called Peach Oak or Pin Oak.

underside

bark

flower

fruit

Silverleaf Oak
Quercus hypoleucoides

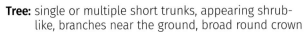

Family: Beech (Fagaceae)

Height: 20–45' (6.1–13.7 m)

Tree: single or multiple short trunks, appearing shrub-like, branches near the ground, broad round crown

Leaf: simple, lance-shaped, 2½–4" (6–10 cm) long, alternately attached, edge sometimes rolled under, no teeth, thick and leathery, yellowish green and shiny above, nearly woolly white or silvery below

Bark: gray, turning light brown with age, thick ridges

Flower: green-to-yellow catkin, 1" (2.5 cm) long, made up of many tiny flowers

Fruit: green acorn, turning brown at maturity, ovate, 1" (2.5 cm) long, solitary or in pairs on a short stalk, turban-shaped cap covering the upper quarter of nut, maturing in 2 seasons

Fall Color: semi-evergreen

Origin/Age: native; 250–350 years

Habitat: rocky soils at elevations above 6,000' (1,830 m), canyons, mountain slopes, oak woodlands, sun

Range: only in the Davis Mountains of Jeff Davis County

Stan's Notes: Can be a shrub or appear like a small tree in Texas, growing to only 20–30 feet (6.1–9.1 m) in high elevations. A highly local tree that is not rare, but not found outside the Davis Mountains. Its simple lance-shaped leaves look nothing like other oak tree leaves. Also known simply as Silverleaf for its leaf underside (see inset). In the species name, *hypo* ("under" or "below") and *leucoides* ("white") describe its leaves. A member of the black (red) oak group, but also called Whiteleaf Oak. Wildlife eat the bitter nuts. Found in Arizona, parts of southwestern New Mexico and the Mexican mountains.

bark

fruit

Live Oak
Quercus virginiana

Family: Beech (Fagaceae)

Height: 30–50' (9.1–15 m)

Tree: medium tree, extremely large single trunk, often divided near the base into multiple large trunks, large dense broad crown up to 100' (30 m) wide

Leaf: simple, oblong, 2–5" (5–13 cm) long, alternately attached, pointed tip with a single bristle, wavy margin, few (if any) teeth, thick, dark green above, paler and with a few hairs to densely hairy below

Bark: dark brown to reddish brown, thick, shallow furrows with flat scales and ridges

Fruit: green acorn, turning brown at maturity, edible, ovate, ¾–1" (2–2.5 cm) long, on a long stalk, cap covering upper half of nut, maturing in 1 season

Fall Color: semi-evergreen

Origin/Age: native; 150–250 years

Habitat: well-drained soils, coastal dunes, often in pure stands, sun

Range: southeastern third of Texas, planted throughout in parks and yards

Stan's Notes: Extremely large, handsome tree with large swooping lower branches that often touch the ground. Considered the ultimate shade tree due to its large spreading horizontal branches. Branches are also home to ferns and other airborne plants (epiphytes). "Live" refers to the leaves, which remain green for most of the year. A fast-growing and long-lived white oak. Susceptible to oak wilt. Native range is a thin strip along the East coast from the Carolinas to Florida and west to Texas. Does not range far from the coast except in Texas.

bark

fruit

Laurel Oak
Quercus laurifolia

Family: Beech (Fagaceae)

Height: 40–60' (12.2–18 m)

Tree: medium tree with a single straight trunk, dense broad round crown

Leaf: simple, lance-shaped to diamond-shaped, 2–5" (5–13 cm) long, alternately attached, pointed tip, wavy toothless margin, shiny bright green above, paler below

Bark: dark brown, thick and smooth when young, becoming deeply furrowed with flat ridges with age

Fruit: green acorn, turning brown to nearly black at maturity, bitter, nearly round, ½–¾" (1–2 cm) long, on a short stalk, shallow scaly cap covering the upper quarter of nut, maturing in 2 seasons

Fall Color: semi-evergreen

Origin/Age: native; 75–100 years

Habitat: moist to wet soils, along rivers and other wet areas, sun to partial shade

Range: southeastern Texas in the Big Thicket area only

Stan's Notes: A relatively fast-growing, short-lived tree known for its dense leaf growth. Widely planted as a shade tree throughout the southern states. Lower branches tend to droop and need pruning to allow for pedestrians. A member of the black (also known as red) oak group. Looking like the Willow Oak (pg. 169) and Water Oak (pg. 177), it is often hard to identify. Usually evergreen, dropping its leaves in spring as new leaves grow. "Laurel" and *laurifolia* refer to its leaves, which resemble the bay leaves of Grecian Laurel (not shown) of the Mediterranean region. Also called Diamondleaf Oak, Darlington Oak and Swamp Laurel Oak.

bark

fruit

Water Oak

Quercus nigra

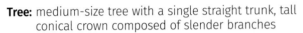

Family: Beech (Fagaceae)

Height: 50–70' (15–21 m)

Tree: medium-size tree with a single straight trunk, tall conical crown composed of slender branches

Leaf: simple, spatulate to wedge-shaped, 2–6" (5–15 cm) long, alternately attached, sometimes 1–3 shallow lobes, widest at the tip, toothless margin, dull blue-green above, paler below, may have tufts of hair along vein angles

Bark: gray to black, thin and smooth, becoming scaly with age

Fruit: green acorn, turning nearly black when mature, ⅓–⅝" (.8–1.5 cm) long, shallow cap, nutmeat is bright orange and bitter, maturing in 2 seasons

Fall Color: yellow to brown, some are semi-evergreen

Origin/Age: native; 75–100 years

Habitat: moist to wet soils, sandy acidic soils, along river floodplains, partial shade to full sun

Range: eastern quarter of Texas, planted in parks, yards and along streets

Stan's Notes: Seen in moist bottomland sites in the eastern quarter of Texas. This oak is unlike the many other oak species that require drier soils. Able to grow with water covering its roots for part of the year. Common name given because it grows in wet areas. Moderate to fast growing, tolerating some shade, doing best in full sun. Easy to propagate, planted in city parks and along streets throughout the South. Prefers sandy acidic soils. Produces acorns after 20 years. A black (red) oak group member, with bitter acorns maturing in their second year. Also called Spotted Oak or Possum Oak.

bark

fruit

Chinquapin Oak
Quercus muehlenbergii

SIMPLE ALTERNATE

Family: Beech (Fagaceae)

Height: 50–70' (15–21 m)

Tree: medium tree, single straight trunk, narrow round crown composed mostly of many short thin twigs

Leaf: simple, 4–6" (10–15 cm) long, alternately attached, with pointed tip, many straight parallel veins, each ending in a curved coarse tooth, shiny dark green above, pale green and slightly hairy below

Bark: light gray to brown, many long narrow scales

Fruit: green acorn, turning brown when mature, ½–1" (1–2.5 cm) long, on a short stalk, cap covering the upper third of nut, maturing in 1 season

Fall Color: red or brown

Origin/Age: native; 100–150 years

Habitat: well-drained deep soils, riverbeds, creek bottoms, along other wet locations, sun

Range: narrow belt from the northeastern corner of Texas southwest to central Texas, isolated pockets in the Trans-Pecos region

Stan's Notes: The leaves of this oak resemble those in a different tree group called chinquapin, hence the common name. Also called Yellow Oak or Chestnut Oak, the latter name referring to the leaf shape, which resembles that of the American Chestnut (not shown). Species name was given in honor of botanist Gotthilf Henry Ernst Muehlenberg (1753–1815). While most other oak trees have lobed leaves, this species has simple leaves of variable size that tend to be gathered at the tips of branches. A member of the white oak group, producing acorns every year unlike the red oak group (also known as black), which produces acorns every other year.

bark

fruit

Swamp Chestnut Oak
Quercus michauxii

SIMPLE ALTERNATE

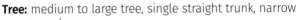

Family: Beech (Fagaceae)

Height: 50–80' (15–24 m)

Tree: medium to large tree, single straight trunk, narrow round crown

Leaf: simple, oval, 4–9" (10–23 cm) long, alternately attached, wavy margin with many coarse rounded teeth, shiny green above, paler with gray-to-green hairs below

Bark: light gray, thick with irregular furrows and scales

Fruit: green acorn, turning brown when mature, edible, egg-shaped (ovate), 1–1½" (2.5–4 cm) long, on a short stalk, thick cap covering the upper third of nut, maturing in 1 season

Fall Color: red to brown

Origin/Age: native; 150–200 years

Habitat: moist soils, floodplains, river valleys, sun to partial shade

Range: far eastern Texas, Pineywoods, Gulf Prairies

Stan's Notes: Known for its large, fuzzy, coarsely toothed leaves and large acorns. "Chestnut" refers to its leaves, which appear similar to the toothed leaves of the American Chestnut (not shown). Sometimes called Cow Oak, presumably because cows eat the acorns. Acorns are also eaten by wildlife such as turkeys, deer and squirrels. Unlike other acorns, these are less bitter and can be eaten without boiling out the tannin. The lumber is hard and strong and has been used in flooring, furniture and tool handles. Baskets have been woven from its wood fibers. Also known as Basket Oak. Given the species name *michauxii* for French naturalist Andre Michaux, who collected plants in the United States during the last half of the eighteenth century.

bark

fruit

Saffron Plum

Sideroxylon celastrinum

Family: Sapodilla (Sapotaceae)

Height: 20–30' (6.1–9.1 m)

Tree: small tree with a short trunk, ascending branches, dense round crown

Leaf: simple, elliptical to oval, 1–1½" (2.5–4 cm) long, alternately to nearly oppositely attached, widest beyond the middle with a long, narrow tapering base, wavy toothless margin, leathery, shiny green above, pale green below

Bark: reddish gray, thin and grooved with many fissures, many stout thorns on branches

Fruit: green berry, turning blue to black when mature, edible, ¾" (2 cm) wide, hanging from a short thin fruit stalk, containing 1 seed

Fall Color: evergreen

Origin/Age: native; 30–50 years

Habitat: coastal wetlands, rocky shores, along rivers and other wetlands well away from the shore, sun

Range: southern tip of Texas, the Rio Grande Valley and up the Gulf coast

Stan's Notes: A small tree that often appears like a tall shrub in the Gulf Prairies and Rio Grande Plains. Found mainly in the southern tip of Texas, extending well into Mexico and also the southern half of Florida. Its evergreen leaves last two or more years. Flowers in May and again in November, with fruit maturing shortly afterward. Fruit is edible and many wildlife species depend on it for food. The wood is light brown, hard and heavy, but has no commercial value. Also known as Tropical Buckthorn and Downward Plum.

fruit

bark

thorn

Chittamwood
Sideroxylon lanuginosum

Family: Sapodilla (Sapotaceae)

Height: 30–50' (9.1–15 m)

Tree: medium tree, nearly straight trunk, stiff branches with stout thorns, narrow pointed crown

Leaf: simple, elliptical to oval, 1–3" (2.5–7.5 cm) long, alternately attached, widest beyond the middle with a long, narrow tapering base, toothless margin, shiny green above, gray and extremely hairy below

Bark: dark gray, many narrow scaly ridges

Fruit: green berry, turning purple to black when mature, edible, ½" (1 cm) wide, hanging from a short thin fruit stalk, containing 1 seed

Fall Color: brown

Origin/Age: native; 30–50 years

Habitat: dry upland soils, along washes, sun to partial shade

Range: eastern three-quarters of Texas

Stan's Notes: This medium-size tree often grows in dense clusters, resembling more of a shrub than a tree. A milky sap oozes from cuts in the trunk and twigs and forms a gum as the sap dries. Children of the early settlers chewed the gum from this tree. Fruit is edible, but ingestion is not recommended since it can cause gastrointestinal upset (stomachache). A relatively pest-free tree, grown as nursery stock. It has a high tolerance for drought and will grow in poor soil, making it a popular landscaping tree. Also known as Woolly Bucket Bumelia, Gum Bumelia, False Buckthorn or Ironwood. The former scientific name was *Bumelia lanuginosa*.

fruit

bark

Siberian Elm
Ulmus pumila

Family: Elm (Ulmaceae)

Height: 30–50' (9.1–15 m)

Tree: single trunk, open irregular crown

Leaf: simple, narrow, ¾–2" (2–5 cm) long, alternately attached, with pointed tip, asymmetrical leaf base, double-toothed margin, dark green

Bark: gray with rough scales

Fruit: flat green disk (samara), lacking hair when young, turning papery brown when mature, ½" (1 cm) wide, with a closed notch opposite fruit stalk

Fall Color: yellow

Origin/Age: non-native, introduced from Asia; 50–75 years

Habitat: wide variety of soils, sun

Range: planted in parks and yards, as hedges, around old home sites, along roadsides

Stan's Notes: A small non-native species that was introduced from Asia. Now found growing along roadsides, old fields, former homesteads and other places where soils were disturbed and people were active. Species name *pumila* means "small" and refers to the small stature. Fast growing, with some of the smallest leaves of any of the elm species. Thrives in a wide variety of soils and tolerates harsh conditions. Somewhat resistant to Dutch elm disease. Can suffer from extensive elm leaf beetle damage every year. Also called Chinese Elm. Another elm species that goes by the same common name, Chinese Elm (*U. parvifolia*) (not shown), is a different, cultivated species.

bark

flower

fruit

Cedar Elm
Ulmus crassifolia

Family: Elm (Ulmaceae)

Height: 50–70' (15–21 m)

Tree: single straight trunk divided high, with spreading branches and a round crown

Leaf: simple, oval, 1–2" (2.5–5 cm) long, alternately attached, widest at the middle, asymmetrical leaf base, pointed or slightly rounded tip, double row of teeth, leathery and rough, dark green above, paler below, on a short leafstalk, ½" (1 cm) long

Bark: light brown to reddish brown and thick, with deep furrows and vertical irregular flat ridges

Flower: bell-shaped red and green flower, ¾" (2 cm) wide, in clusters

Fruit: green disk (samara), turning brown with long white hairs on the edge when mature, rounded, ½" (1 cm) long, with a notched tip opposite the fruit stalk

Fall Color: yellow

Origin/Age: native; 125–150 years

Habitat: rich moist soils, along streams, slopes, sun

Range: eastern quarter of Texas, isolated pockets extend into the panhandle, planted in parks and yards

Stan's Notes: This species has the smallest leaves of all native elms. Found from northern Mexico through eastern Texas into southern Oklahoma, northern Louisiana and Arkansas. Often in bottomlands by streams and rivers, where there is constant water. Fast growing, planted for shade. Flowers from August to October. Fruit ripens in November. Wildlife eat the fruit when little else is available. Named "Cedar" since it often grows with cedar and juniper trees. Species name *crassifolia* means "thick leaves." Susceptible to mistletoe.

189

bark

fruit

winged twig

Winged Elm
Ulmus alata

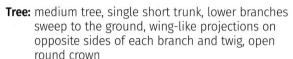

Family: Elm (Ulmaceae)

Height: 30–50' (9.1–15 m)

Tree: medium tree, single short trunk, lower branches sweep to the ground, wing-like projections on opposite sides of each branch and twig, open round crown

Leaf: simple, oval, 1½–3½" (4–9 cm) long, alternately attached, asymmetrical leaf base, double-toothed margin, pointed tip, slightly rough, thick and firm, dark green above, paler with grayish hairs below

Bark: dark gray, deeply furrowed with flat ridges, corky and scaly

Flower: tiny reddish flower, ¼" (.6 cm) wide, in clusters, 1" (2.5 cm) wide

Fruit: flat, fuzzy green disk (samara), turning reddish at maturity, oval, ¼" (.6 cm) wide, notched tip opposite the fruit stalk, long silver hairs along margin

Fall Color: yellow

Origin/Age: native; 50–100 years

Habitat: wide variety of soils, from wet to dry and sandy to clay, sun to partial shade

Range: eastern quarter of Texas, planted in parks, yards

Stan's Notes: An easy tree to identify by its corky winged branches and twigs (see inset), but size of wings can be highly variable. Occurs in a variety of habitats from wet river valleys to dry rocky outcrops. Popular for planting because it is so adaptable. A sturdy species that grows well in urban areas such as along streets. Susceptible to Dutch elm disease. Also called Cork Elm, Wahoo Elm or Witch Elm.

bark

fruit

Water Elm
Planera aquatica

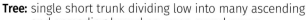

Family: Elm (Ulmaceae)

Height: 30–50' (9.1–15 m)

Tree: single short trunk dividing low into many ascending and spreading branches, open round crown

Leaf: simple, oval, 2–3½" (5–9 cm) long, alternately attached, widest near the base, asymmetrical base, pointed tip, coarse teeth, dark green above, paler below, on a very short leafstalk, ⅛" (.3 cm) long

Bark: gray to light brown, thin and smooth, becoming deeply furrowed with age

Fruit: warty green fruit (drupe), turning light-colored at maturity, ⅜" (.9 cm) wide, on a short fruit stalk, containing 1 seed

Fall Color: yellow

Origin/Age: native; 100–125 years

Habitat: moist soils, wet soils, along streams and rivers, swamps, floodplains and other wetlands, sun

Range: scattered in isolated pockets in far eastern Texas, upper Gulf coast

Stan's Notes: A fairly uncommon tree, especially in Texas. Ranges from Georgia and Florida across the Gulf coast, reaching its western limits in eastern Texas. Always associated with water, in swamps, floodplains, along rivers and streams. One of the few tree species that can thrive in shallow standing water for long periods of time. Slow growing and short lived. It is the only species in its genus and is not well studied. The name *Planera* comes from a dedication to the late German botanist, Jakob Planer (1743–89).

bark

flower

fruit

American Elm
Ulmus americana

Family: Elm (Ulmaceae)

Height: 70–100' (21–30 m)

Tree: one of the tallest trees, single trunk, prominent root flares, upper limbs fan out gracefully, forming an upright vase shape, branch tips often drooping

Leaf: simple, oval, 3–6" (7.5–15 cm) long, alternately attached, with pointed tip, asymmetrical leaf base, double-toothed margin, slightly rough to touch, only 2–3 forked veins per leaf

Bark: dark gray, deeply furrowed with flat ridges, corky, sometimes scaly

Flower: tiny reddish brown flower, ¼" (.6 cm) diameter, in clusters, 1" (2.5 cm) wide

Fruit: flat, fuzzy green disk (samara), turning tan when mature, round to oval, ½" (1 cm) diameter, with a notch opposite the fruit stalk

Fall Color: yellow

Origin/Age: native; 150–200 years

Habitat: moist soils, full sun

Range: eastern third of Texas except the far south, planted in parks, yards, along city streets and parkways

Stan's Notes: This once dominant tree lined just about every city street in eastern North America, but this is not nearly the case in Texas. Almost eliminated due to Dutch elm disease, which is caused by a fungus that attacks the vascular system of the tree. The fungus was introduced to the United States in the 1920s by infected elm logs from Europe. Its arching branches form a canopy, providing shade. The distinct vase shape of the mature tree makes it easy to recognize from a distance. Also called White Elm.

bark

fruit

Slippery Elm
Ulmus rubra

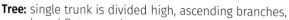

Family: Elm (Ulmaceae)

Height: 50–70' (15–21 m)

Tree: single trunk is divided high, ascending branches, broad flat-topped crown

Leaf: simple, oval, 4–7" (10–18 cm) long, alternately attached, widest above the middle, asymmetrical leaf base, approximately 26–30 veins, some forked near the margin, rough and dark green above, paler below, on a short leafstalk

Bark: brown to reddish brown, shallow furrows, vertical irregular flat scales, inner bark reddish

Fruit: green disk (samara), turning brown when mature, nearly round, ½–¾" (1–2 cm) in diameter, with a slightly notched tip opposite the fruit stalk, few reddish brown hairs

Fall Color: yellow

Origin/Age: native; 100–125 years

Habitat: rich moist soils, along streams, slopes, sun

Range: northeastern quarter of Texas

Stan's Notes: Due to its habit of growing near water, sometimes is called Water Elm. More often called Red Elm because of its reddish inner bark. The inner bark is fragrant and mucilaginous, hence its common name "Slippery." Scientific name used to be *U. fulva*. The inner bark was once chewed to quench thirst and used to cure sore throats. Leaves are smaller than those of most other elm species and feel rough. Look for forked veins near the margin. Leaf buds are dark rusty brown and covered with hairs, making the tree easy to identify even without leaves. Smaller than the American Elm (pg. 195), lacks the distinct vase shape and not as common in Texas.

thorn

bark

fruit

Desert Hackberry

Celtis pallida

Family: Hemp (Cannabaceae)

Height: 10–15' (3–4.6 m)

Tree: small tree to large shrub with a single trunk that is often crooked, densely branched, zigzag branches with many thorns, irregular spreading crown

Leaf: simple, oval, 1–2" (2.5–5 cm) long, alternately attached, smooth margin or wavy with few teeth, thick, dark green above, paler below with hairs on conspicuous net-like veins

Bark: gray, smooth, covered with irregular warty bumps

Flower: tiny green-to-white flower, ⅛" (.3 cm) wide, sprouting from the base of leaves in early spring

Fruit: green berry-like fleshy fruit (drupe), turning yellow to orange at maturity, sweet and edible when ripe, ¼" (.6 cm) wide, hanging from a long fruit stalk, containing 1 seed

Fall Color: semi-evergreen

Origin/Age: native; 100–500 years

Habitat: dry soils, hillsides, along streams, sun

Range: southwestern corner of Texas

Stan's Notes: Also called Spiny Hackberry or Granjeno. Common in foothills; sometimes planted as an ornamental tree in parks and yards. An extremely drought-resistant semi-evergreen seen in southwestern Texas, ranging naturally across Mexico into South America. Single thorns or thorn pairs grow opposite leaves; deer and cattle eat the leaves despite the thorns. Birds and mammals enjoy the fruit. Flowers are in elongated clusters. Berries appear in late fall, flowers in late winter. Host for some butterfly caterpillar species.

bark

fruit

Netleaf Hackberry
Celtis laevigata reticulata

Family: Hemp (Cannabaceae)

Height: 10–30' (3–9.1 m)

Tree: small tree with a single trunk that is frequently crooked, irregular spreading crown

Leaf: simple, lance-shaped, 1–3" (2.5–7.5 cm) long, alternately attached, long tapering tip, asymmetrical leaf base, smooth margin or wavy with a few teeth, thick, dark green above, paler with hairs on conspicuous net-like veins below

Bark: gray, corky, covered with irregular wart-like bumps

Flower: tiny green flower, ⅛" (.3 cm) wide, sprouting from the base of young leaves in early spring

Fruit: green berry-like fleshy fruit (drupe), turning reddish brown to orange when mature, sweet and edible when ripe, ¼" (.6 cm) wide, hanging from a long fruit stalk, containing 1 seed

Fall Color: yellow

Origin/Age: native; 75–100 years

Habitat: dry soils up to 6,000' (1,830 m), rocky ravines, canyons, hillsides, along streams, sun

Range: scattered widely across north central and western Texas, planted in parks and yards

Stan's Notes: Easy to identify by its unique corky bark. Slow growing and deep-rooted, able to grow in dry areas and survive drought. Good to plant along driveways and sidewalks because it has minimal impact on hard surfaces. Reproduces well by seed. Mature trees are laden with fruit in fall. Fruit is often eaten by birds during winter. Brown-to-red dye is extracted from leaves and branches. Wood is not strong; not used commercially. Also called Western Hackberry.

immature
fruit

bark

flower

fruit

Hackberry
Celtis occidentalis

Family: Hemp (Cannabaceae)

Height: 40–60' (12.2–18 m)

Tree: single trunk, ascending branches with drooping tips, spreading round crown

Leaf: simple, lance-shaped, 2–4" (5–10 cm) long, alternately attached, long tapering tip, asymmetrical leaf base, evenly spaced sharp teeth, hairs on the veins, dark green above, paler below

Bark: unique gray bark with thin corky ridges, wart-like

Flower: tiny green flower, ⅛" (.3 cm) wide, sprouting from the base of young leaves in early spring

Fruit: green berry-like fruit (drupe), turning deep purple, sweet and edible when ripe, ¼" (.6 cm) wide, 1 seed

Fall Color: yellow

Origin/Age: native; 100–150 years

Habitat: wide variety of soils, partial shade

Range: only Hemphill County in the panhandle, planted in parks and yards

Stan's Notes: Unique corky bark makes this tree easy to identify. Similar to Netleaf Hackberry (pg. 201) and Sugarberry (pg. 205). In autumn, mature trees are laden with dark purple berry-like fruit, which typically doesn't last long since it is a favorite food of many bird species. Fruit can remain on trees through winter if not eaten by birds. Suffers from witches'-broom, a non-fatal condition caused by combined efforts of an insect and a fungus that results in dense clusters of small short twigs at ends of branches. Often has dimple-like galls on leaves (which do not affect tree health) caused by mites. Susceptible to mistletoe. Also called Hacktree, Northern Hackberry or Sugarberry.

bark

immature fruit

fruit

Sugarberry
Celtis laevigata

SIMPLE ALTERNATE

Family: Elm (Ulmaceae)

Height: 60–80' (18–24 m)

Tree: single tall straight trunk, slightly drooping lower branches, open round crown

Leaf: simple, lance-shaped, 2–5" (5–13 cm) long, alternately attached, long and pointed, often curved tip, asymmetrical leaf base, toothless to fine teeth, dark green and smooth above, paler below

Bark: light brown to gray or silver, thin and smooth when young, becoming very corky with many warts in an irregular pattern with age

Flower: tiny green flower, ⅛" (.3 cm) wide, sprouting from the base of young leaves in early spring

Fruit: green berry-like fruit (drupe), turning orange red to dark blue at maturity, sweet and edible when ripe, ¼" (.6 cm) wide, on a long fruit stalk, 1 seed

Fall Color: yellow

Origin/Age: native; 100–150 years

Habitat: moist soils, river valleys, usually understory of mixed deciduous trees, sometimes in pure stands, partial shade to sun

Range: eastern half of Texas with the exception of the far south, planted in parks and yards

Stan's Notes: Similar to Hackberry (pg. 203), but differentiated by longer, narrower, smoother leaves with toothless margins. Bark has a more irregular pattern of warts, and trunk has more smooth open patches than Hackberry. Often planted for shade, as an accent tree or to attract birds. Birds love the fruit, often stripping immature fruit (see inset) from trees. Also called Sugar Hackberry or Hackberry.

bark

Knowlton Hophornbeam

Ostrya knowltonii

Family: Birch (Betulaceae)

Height: 10–25' (3–7.6 m)

Tree: small tree with a short single trunk, often branching or with several smaller crooked trunks dividing close to the ground, regular round crown

Leaf: simple, oval or round, 1–2" (2.5–5 cm) long and 1–1½" (2.5–4 cm) wide, alternately attached, may have a pointed tip, fine-toothed edge, dull green above, lighter below

Bark: gray to brown and thick, breaking into loose scales with age

Fruit: green sac-like structure, turning tan and papery when mature, 1–1½" (2.5–4 cm) long, each sac containing a flattened seed (nutlet), ¼" (.6 cm) long

Fall Color: yellow

Origin/Age: native; 50–100 years

Habitat: dry rocky soils, sandy soils between 5,000-9000' (1,525-2,745 m); canyons, sun

Range: Guadalupe Mountains only, northern Trans-Pecos

Stan's Notes: An extremely uncommon tree, growing in protected canyons. Not in abundance anywhere in its range from the extreme northern Trans-Pecos to parts of New Mexico, northwestern Arizona and southern Utah. Also called Western Hophornbeam, it is similar to Eastern Hophornbeam (not shown), differing only by the size of the fruit. The bladder-like fruit appears like hops and is used to brew beer, hence the common name. Stinging hairs cover the fruit so use caution whenever handling. Wood from this tree is very heavy and hard. The genus name *Ostrya* comes from the Greek word *ostrua* for "bone-like" and refers to the hardness of the wood.

mature fruit

bark

flower

immature fruit

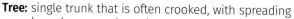

Ironwood
Ostrya virginiana

Family: Birch (Betulaceae)

Height: 20–40' (6.1–12.2 m)

Tree: single trunk that is often crooked, with spreading branches, open irregular crown

Leaf: simple, oval, 2–4" (5–10 cm) long, alternately attached, with a pointed tip and asymmetrical leaf base, double-toothed margin, fuzzy, yellow green

Bark: gray, fibrous with narrow ridges spiraling around the trunk

Flower: catkin, ½–1" (1–2.5 cm) long

Fruit: flattened nutlet, ¼" (.6 cm) wide, within a hanging cluster of inflated sacs that are green when young, turning brown at maturity, 1½–2" (4–5 cm) long, appearing like the fruit of the hop plant

Fall Color: yellow

Origin/Age: native; 75–100 years

Habitat: dry soils, slopes, ridges, shade tolerant

Range: eastern edge in Pineywoods

Stan's Notes: An important understory tree, frequently spending its entire life in the shade of other taller trees. The common name refers to its very strong and heavy wood, which is used to make tool handles and tent stakes. Distinctive thin scaly bark that spirals up the trunk and velvety soft leaves make this tree easy to identify. Also called Hophornbeam in direct reference to its fruit sacs, which look like hops. One of three species of *Ostrya* in North America.

bark

flower

fruit

Texas Persimmon
Diospyros texana

Family: Ebony (Ebenaceae)

Height: 10–40' (3–12.2 m)

Tree: small to medium tree, single trunk dividing low with many short branches, broad crown

Leaf: simple, oval to elliptical, 1–2" (2.5–5 cm) long, alternately attached, with a rounded tip, narrow at the base, lacking teeth, leathery, dark green above, lighter below with many white hairs

Bark: gray to light reddish gray, smooth and peeling to expose smooth gray-to-pink inner bark

Flower: 5–lobed, bell-shaped white-to-cream flower, ½" (1 cm) long, in pairs or groups at base of leafstalk

Fruit: green fleshy berry, turning black at maturity, thick-skinned, sweet, juicy and edible, 1" (2.5 cm) wide, on a short fruit stalk, containing 3–8 seeds

Fall Color: semi-evergreen

Origin/Age: native; 150–200 years

Habitat: wide variety of soils, desert scrub, river valleys, upland woodland sites

Range: southern half of Texas excluding the upper Gulf coast and far western Texas, planted in parks and yards in the southern half of Texas

Stan's Notes: Usually does not grow above 10 feet (3 m) in Texas. Male and female flowers occur on separate plants (dioecious); male plants far outnumber female, which produce fruit. Often evergreen in the southern part of its range, dropping its leaves farther north. Many seeds in the ripe black fruit make it difficult to eat. Planted in landscapes because of its attractive gray bark. Also called Mexican Persimmon, Black Persimmon and Chapote.

immature fruit

bark

flower

fruit

Common Persimmon

Diospyros virginiana

Family: Ebony (Ebenaceae)

Height: 30–40' (9.1–12.2 m)

Tree: small to medium tree, single straight trunk, many short branches, dense cylindrical crown

Leaf: simple, oval to elliptical, 2–6" (5–15 cm) long, alternately attached, pointed tip, smooth margin, shiny dark green above, whitish green below

Bark: brown to nearly black, thick and deeply furrowed into small squares

Flower: 4–lobed, bell-shaped white-to-cream flower, ½–¾" (1–2 cm) long, solitary at the base of leafstalk

Fruit: green fleshy berry, turning orange to purplish brown when mature, edible, ¾–1½" (2–4 cm) wide, on a short fruit stalk, many flat brown seeds

Fall Color: yellow

Origin/Age: native; 100–200 years

Habitat: wide variety of soils, river valleys, dry upland woodland sites, mixed forests, shade tolerant

Range: eastern quarter of Texas from the Pineywoods and Post Oak Savannah to the prairies of central Texas

Stan's Notes: An interesting tree, often planted for its glossy leaves and attractive square-patterned bark. Slow growing, able to live in understory many years. Not easily transplanted due to its large taproot. Known for its fruit, which ripens in autumn only after a couple freeze-thaw cycles. Ripe fruit, tasting like dates, is used in puddings, cakes and bread. Closely related to the persimmons sold in stores. Wood is close-grained and hard, used for billiard cues and golf club heads. One of two native members of the Ebony family, which has over 400 worldwide. Also called Date Plum or Possumwood.

bark

flower

fruit

Quaking Aspen
Populus tremuloides

SIMPLE
ALTERNATE

Family: Willow (Salicaceae)

Height: 40–70' (12.2–21 m)

Tree: slender tree with a straight trunk, round crown

Leaf: simple, nearly round, 1–3" (2.5–7.5 cm) long, alternately attached, with short sharp point, fine-toothed margin, shiny green above and dull green below, leafstalk (petiole) flattened

Bark: dark gray to brown and deeply furrowed lower, greenish white to cream and smooth upper

Flower: catkin, 1–2" (2.5–5 cm) long, male and female bloom (flower) on separate trees (dioecious) in spring before the leaves bud

Fruit: catkin-like fruit, 4" (10 cm) long, made of many tiny green capsules, ⅛" (.3 cm) long, that open and release seeds, seeds are attached to cottony white material and float on the wind

Fall Color: golden yellow

Origin/Age: native; 60–80 years

Habitat: wet or dry, sandy or rocky soils above elevations of 7,000' (2,135 m), sun

Range: Chisos, Davis and Guadalupe Mountains in the Trans-Pecos, planted in parks and yards

Stan's Notes: The most widely distributed tree in North America. Leaves catch gentle breezes and shake or quake in wind. Also known as Trembling Aspen or Popple. Grows in large, often pure stands. Returns from roots if cut or toppled. Most reproduce by suckering off their roots, which creates clone trees. One stand in Utah–106 acres (42 ha) with about 47,000 trees–is the heaviest single living organism in the world. Has survived lab temperatures of -314°F (-192°C).

bark

flower

fruit

Rio Grande Cottonwood
Populus deltoides wislizeni

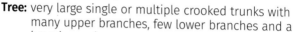

Family: Willow (Salicaceae)

Height: 70–100' (21–30 m)

Tree: very large single or multiple crooked trunks with many upper branches, few lower branches and a broad round crown

Leaf: simple, triangular, 2–3½" (5–9 cm) long, alternately attached, with fine to medium teeth, thin and firm, bright yellow green above, paler below, leafstalk slender and somewhat flattened

Bark: gray with deep flat furrows lower, greenish yellow and smooth upper

Flower: catkin, 3–6" (7.5–15 cm) long

Fruit: catkin-like fruit, 3" (7.5 cm) long, composed of many tiny ovate capsules, ¼" (.6 cm) long, that split open into 2 parts and release seeds, seeds are attached to cotton-like filaments and float on wind

Fall Color: yellow to gold

Origin/Age: native; 100–150 years

Habitat: moist soils, by streams, wetlands, sun to shade

Range: scattered in the far western part of Texas in the Trans-Pecos region, planted in parks and yards

Stan's Notes: One of the largest trees in western North America, with a massive trunk. Crown may be as wide as the tree is tall. Hardy and fast growing, almost always near water and often in dense stands by rivers. Also called Fremont Cottonwood, Valley Cottonwood or Alamo Cottonwood. Leaves turn color when fall temperatures drop gradually; leaves drop without changing color when weather cools suddenly. Wood has been used for fence posts and firewood. Indigenous peoples used parts of the tree to make baskets, tools and drums.

Plains Cottonwood

bark

flower

seeds

Eastern Cottonwood
Populus deltoides

Family: Willow (Salicaceae)

Height: 70–100' (21–30 m)

Tree: large tree with single or multiple trunks, few lower branches and a huge, broad irregular crown

Leaf: simple, triangular, 3–6" (7.5–15 cm) long, alternately attached, coarse-toothed margin, thick and waxy, shiny green, leafstalk long and flattened

Bark: gray with deep flat furrows

Flower: catkin, 2–3" (5–7.5 cm) long

Fruit: catkin-like fruit, 4" (10 cm) long, made of many tiny ovate capsules, ¼" (.6 cm) long, that split open into 4 parts and release seeds (see inset), seeds are attached to cotton-like filaments and float on wind

Fall Color: yellow

Origin/Age: native; 50–200 years

Habitat: wet soils, along streams, rivers and lakes, sun

Range: eastern half of Texas, planted in wet areas

Stan's Notes: A huge tree of riverbanks, floodplains and other wet areas. Some trees can obtain heights of 150 feet (50 m), with trunk diameters of 7–8 feet (2.1–2.4 m). Fast growing, up to 5 feet (1.5 m) in height and over 1 inch (2.5 cm) in diameter per year. The species name *deltoides* is Latin, describing the delta-shaped leaf. Known for the massive release of seed-bearing "cotton," hence the common name "Cottonwood." Several subspecies of Eastern Cottonwood are found in Texas. The Plains Cottonwood (*P. d. occidentalis*) (see inset), essentially a smaller version of Eastern Cottonwood, occurs in the panhandle and can tolerate drier soils.

bark

flower

fruit

Mexican Plum
Prunus mexicana

SIMPLE ALTERNATE

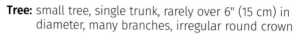

Family: Rose (Rosaceae)

Height: 15–25' (4.6–7.6 m)

Tree: small tree, single trunk, rarely over 6" (15 cm) in diameter, many branches, irregular round crown

Leaf: simple, oval to oblong, 2–4" (5–10 cm) long, alternately attached, with a pointed tip, double row of fine teeth, smooth, shiny and dark yellow-green above, paler below and hairy along the veins

Bark: reddish brown, smooth when young, becoming scaly with age

Flower: 5–petaled showy white flower, ½" (1 cm) wide, in clusters of 2–4, fragrant

Fruit: large green fleshy plum (drupe), turning red to purple when mature, with a whitish powdery coating, edible, 1" (2.5 cm) wide, with 1 large seed

Fall Color: golden yellow

Origin/Age: native; 25–30 years

Habitat: wide variety of soils from wet to dry, open fields, woodland edges, fencerows, river bottoms, forests, shade intolerant

Range: eastern half of Texas, planted in parks and yards

Stan's Notes: Fairly common in many soils and habitats. Drought tolerant, planted by many in landscapes. Flowers before the leaves appear, making it attractive. Plums are prized by wildlife and people. Plums make good jellies and jams and can be eaten fresh. Crushed twigs often smell of bitter almond. Two other plum species in Texas: Munson Plum (*P. munsoniana*), a smaller tree with narrower leaves, is rare in Texas; Murray Plum (*P. murrayana*) was discovered in 1928, but only a few scattered individuals occur in Texas today.

flower

bark

fruit

Laurel Cherry
Prunus caroliniana

Family: Rose (Rosaceae)

Height: 20–40' (6.1–12.2 m)

Tree: single or multiple thin trunks, broad round crown

Leaf: simple, lance-shaped, 2–5" (5–13 cm) long, alternately attached, pointed tip, smooth margin or with a few fine teeth, smooth and leathery, dark green above, paler below

Bark: gray, thin and smooth, becoming rough and with shallow fissures with age

Flower: 5–petaled white flower, ½" (1 cm) diameter, many flowers in elongated clusters, 2–4" (5–10 cm) long

Fruit: green cherry (drupe), dark blue or black when mature, edible, ¼–½" (.6–1 cm) wide, in clusters

Fall Color: evergreen

Origin/Age: native; 125–150 years

Habitat: moist soils, dry soils, river bottoms, hedgerows, fencerows, partial shade to sun

Range: eastern edge of Texas, planted in parks and yards

Stan's Notes: A fast-growing, short-lived small to medium cherry tree of the eastern United States from the Carolinas to Florida and west to Texas. Early in the 1900s it was planted in landscapes across Texas for its evergreen leaves and shiny edible fruit. After a severe drought in the 1950s and an ensuing infestation of insect borers, most of the trees died. It was never replanted and today only a few stands of mature trees are seen in older landscapes and abandoned homesteads. Now often planted in northern Texas. Hydrocyanic acid within the leaves reacts with stomach acids and releases cyanide, which can kill animals that eat the leaves.

midrib hairs

immature fruit

bark

flower

fruit

Black Cherry
Prunus serotina

Family: Rose (Rosaceae)

Height: 25–50' (7.6–15 m)

Tree: straight tree, single trunk, showing little tapering, often tilted or bent, with few lower branches and many upper branches, open round crown

Leaf: simple, lance-shaped, 2–6" (5–15 cm) long, alternately attached, with a unique inward-curved tip resembling a bird's beak, fine-toothed margin, row of fine brown hairs along the midrib underneath (see inset), shiny dark green above, paler below

Bark: dark reddish brown to black in color with large, conspicuous curving scales (like potato chips), green inner bark tastes bitter, but smells pleasant

Flower: white flower, ½" (1 cm) wide, 6–12 per elongated cluster, 4–6" (10–15 cm) long

Fruit: green cherry (drupe), red to dark blue or black at maturity, edible, ¼–½" (.6–1 cm) wide, in clusters

Fall Color: yellow

Origin/Age: native; 125–150 years

Habitat: moist and dry soils, mixed with deciduous species, partial shade to sun

Range: eastern quarter of Texas, Trans-Pecos region and isolated in central Texas, planted in parks, yards

Stan's Notes: Widely sought for its rich brown wood for furniture and cabinets. Its tart fruit is an important food for wildlife. Bark and roots have hydrocyanic acid, used in cough medicines. Black knot fungus, its most common disease, results in growths on twigs and branches, leading to die-back. Flowers in March in eastern Texas and in April in western Texas. Several subspecies grow in Texas.

bark

Peachleaf Willow
Salix amygdaloides

Family: Willow (Salicaceae)

Height: 30–50' (9.1–15 m)

Tree: medium tree, single or multiple crooked trunks, upright branches, broad round crown

Leaf: simple, narrow lance-shaped, 2–4" (5–10 cm) long, alternately attached, fine-toothed margin, thin and firm, light green above, paler to nearly white below, on a long leafstalk (petiole)

Bark: dark brown to reddish brown, irregular furrows with broad flat ridges

Flower: catkin, 1½–3" (4–7.5 cm) long

Fruit: catkin-like fruit, 1–2" (2.5–5 cm) long, composed of many capsules, each ¼" (.6 cm) long, hanging in clusters on a long fruit stalk

Fall Color: pale green to yellow

Origin/Age: native; 50–75 years

Habitat: moist to wet soils in low elevations, along streams, marshes, wet meadows and other wet areas, sun

Range: top of the Texas panhandle, scattered in the Trans-Pecos, planted as shelterbelts

Stan's Notes: A hardy, fast-growing tree that often forms thickets along streams and other wet areas. Frequently associated with other water-loving trees such as cottonwoods. Planted as shelterbelts to help stabilize wet soils near shores. Twigs are flexible and can be bent into a circle without breaking. Leaves often remain on the tree through autumn. The species name *amygdaloides*, from *amygdalus*, meaning "peach," refers to the leaves, which look like those of a peach tree. Also called Almond Willow.

bark

fruit

Black Willow
Salix nigra

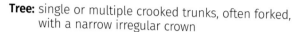

Family: Willow (Salicaceae)

Height: 40–60' (12.2–18 m)

Tree: single or multiple crooked trunks, often forked, with a narrow irregular crown

Leaf: simple, narrow lance-shaped, 3–6" (7.5–15 cm) long, alternately attached, fine-toothed margin, shiny green, on a short leafstalk, often with tiny leaf-like appendages (stipules) that make the leaf appear to be clasping the twig

Bark: dark brown and deeply furrowed into large patchy scales with flat-topped ridges

Flower: catkin, 2–3" (5–7.5 cm) long, hanging down

Fruit: catkin-like fruit, 2–3" (5–7.5 cm) long, composed of many capsules, ¼" (.6 cm) long, seeds within

Fall Color: light yellow

Origin/Age: native; 50–75 years

Habitat: wet soils, stream banks, wetlands and other wet places, shade intolerant

Range: throughout Texas except for the upper panhandle

Stan's Notes: The largest and most widespread native willow in Texas. Common name "Black" is for the dark bark. A fast-growing, short-lived tree that does not tolerate shade. Commonly found along streams, rivers and other wet places. Also known as Swamp Willow. Twigs are light yellow to reddish and downy when young, becoming gray and hairless. Branches are spreading and easily broken by high winds. Look for its large leaves and leaf-like stipules to help identify.

bark

flower

fruit

Desert Willow
Chilopsis linearis

Family: Trumpet-creeper (Bignoniaceae)

Height: 20–25' (6.1–7.6 m)

Tree: large shrub to small tree with short twisted trunks, broad round crown

Leaf: simple, narrow lance-shaped, 6–8" (15–20 cm) long, alternately attached, smooth wavy margin, light green, on a short leafstalk (petiole)

Bark: light gray to dark gray with many wide flat ridges and flakes

Flower: large white-to-pink and red tubular flower, 1–2" (2.5–5 cm) long

Fruit: long, narrow green seedpods, turning brown with age, 4–8" (10–20 cm) long, ¼" wide, seeds within

Fall Color: yellow

Origin/Age: native; 75–150 years

Habitat: dry gravel soils, along washes, rivers and streams, grasslands, sun

Range: western Texas, planted in parks and yards

Stan's Notes: This tree is not a true willow. Related to the Southern Catalpa (pg. 87), which has similar flowers and seedpods. Ranges from southern California across Arizona and into southern portions of New Mexico, western Texas and well into Mexico. Almost always in desert washes and grasslands in low elevations. Reaches its largest size when growing near a constant or good water supply; otherwise stays small and inconspicuous. It flowers from April through August. May have fruit at the same time. Planted for its showy flowers and pretty fruit. Also called Flowering Willow, False Willow, Willowleaf Catalpa, Mimbre or Jano. Species *linearis* refers to its linear leaves.

bark

flower

fruit

Texas Mulberry
Morus microphylla

SIMPLE ALTERNATE

Family: Mulberry (Moraceae)

Height: 10–20' (3–6.1 m)

Tree: small tree to large shrub with a single trunk, often dividing low, open round crown

Leaf: lobed, multi-lobed to oval, ½–2" (1–5 cm) long, alternately attached, pointed tip and coarse teeth, exudes milky sap when torn, dull green and rough above, paler and smooth below, somewhat hairy

Bark: light gray to reddish brown and smooth, becoming furrowed with age

Flower: many tiny green flowers, each ¼" (.6 cm) wide, in clusters, 1" (2.5 cm) long

Fruit: red berry (aggregate fruit), turning black, looking raspberry-like, made of many tiny 1–seeded fruit, sweet to sour and edible, ½" (1 cm) wide

Fall Color: yellow

Origin/Age: native; 50–75 years

Habitat: gravelly soils at 2,200–6,500' (670–1,980 m), along streams in protected canyons, grasslands, sun

Range: scattered in the western half of Texas

Stan's Notes: One of two native mulberries in Texas. Different from Red Mulberry (pg. 237) by its overall size. Range extends from Texas to Oklahoma, New Mexico and Arizona. Also known as Western Mulberry, Mexican Mulberry, Small-leaved Mulberry and Mountain Mulberry. Blooms in early spring (April). Male flowers on one tree, female flowers on another (dioecious). Only female flowers produce fruit, which matures during late summer. Animals and birds eat the berries, coming from miles around to feed. Wood is hard and heavy. Leaf shape varies somewhat from tree to tree.

bark

fruit

White Mulberry
Morus alba

Family: Mulberry (Moraceae)

Height: 10–30' (3–9.1 m)

Tree: small tree with a single trunk, often dividing low, with an open round crown

Leaf: simple, oval to multi-lobed, 2–5" (5–13 cm) long, alternately attached, with a coarse-toothed edge, exuding milky sap when torn, shiny green above, hairy tufts below

Bark: orange brown, deeply furrowed with flat ridges

Fruit: pink, purple or white berry (aggregate fruit) with a raspberry-like appearance, made of many tiny 1–seeded fruit, sweet and edible, ½" (1 cm) wide

Fall Color: yellow

Origin/Age: non-native, introduced to the United States from Russia and China; 50–75 years

Habitat: dry soils, old fields, protected canyons, old ranch sites, sun

Range: planted in parks and yards, along roads, near old home sites

Stan's Notes: Also called Russian Mulberry or Silkworm Mulberry. Produces abundant berries, which attract birds from miles around. In July and August, when fruit is ripe, the tree is full of activity with birds, squirrels and other animals and the ground is often covered with fallen berries. Usually grows along fencerows, where perching birds pass the seeds through their digestive tracts unharmed. Leaves exude a milky sap when torn or cut. White Mulberry was introduced in colonial times in an attempt to build a silkworm industry, with large groves planted in eastern and southwestern states.

fruit

bark

Red Mulberry
Morus rubra

Family: Mulberry (Moraceae)

Height: 20–30' (6.1–9.1 m)

Tree: single trunk divided low, with spreading branches and a dense round crown

Leaf: simple, oval to multi-lobed, 2–5" (5–13 cm) long, alternately attached, with a coarse-toothed margin, exudes milky sap when torn, shiny green above, hairy tufts below

Bark: gray to reddish brown with uneven furrows

Fruit: green berry (aggregate fruit), turning red to black, appearing like a raspberry, made up of many tiny 1–seeded fruit, sweet and edible, ½" (1 cm) wide

Fall Color: yellow

Origin/Age: native; 50–75 years

Habitat: moist soils, floodplains, river valleys, sun to partial shade

Range: eastern two-thirds of Texas, formerly planted in parks and yards

Stan's Notes: This species produces large crops of fruit, providing an important food source for wildlife, especially birds. In summer, berries ripen to red and are delicious when black. Fruit is sweet and juicy and used in jams, jellies and pies. New trees are started when seeds pass through the digestive tracts of birds unharmed and are deposited. Its common name and the species name *rubra* refer to its mostly red fruit. Early settlers and American Indians used its fresh fruit to make beverages, cakes and preserves, and medicinally to cure dysentery and other ailments. Used to be planted in parks and yards, but fell out of favor due to the overabundance of fruit.

bark

Black Tupelo
Nyssa sylvatica

SIMPLE ALTERNATE

Family: Dogwood (Cornaceae)

Height: 50–70' (15–21 m)

Tree: narrow conical tree, single trunk, many slender, often horizontal branches, round crown

Leaf: simple, oval, 2–5" (5–13 cm) long, alternately attached, usually widest above center of leaf, wavy toothless margin, shiny green above, paler and often hairy below, leafstalk often red, leaves often clustered at ends of branches

Bark: light gray to light brown, flaky texture with thick, irregular rectangular ridges

Fruit: green berry-like fruit (drupe), turning blue-black when mature, ½" (1 cm) wide, containing 1 seed

Fall Color: red

Origin/Age: native; 50–100 years

Habitat: moist to wet soils, by streams or wetlands, partial shade

Range: eastern edge of Texas, Pineywoods, Gulf Prairies

Stan's Notes: A common species throughout the eastern United States from New England to Florida and west to the eastern edge of Texas. This is a medium-size tree, often planted as an ornamental for its red leaves in autumn and its fruit, which birds and mammals eat when ripe, also in the fall. In southern states, bees collect nectar from its flowers during spring and produce Tupelo honey. Also called Blackgum, Sourgum and Pepperidge. Reproduces by sprouts growing from its roots. The genus name *Nyssa*, derived from *nysa*, meaning "water nymph," originally described another Nyssa species that occurs in swamps, the Water Tupelo (p. 215). Species name *sylvatica* means "of the woods" and describes the habitat.

bark

immature fruit

Water Tupelo
Nyssa aquatica

Family: Dogwood (Cornaceae)

Height: 80–100' (24–30 m)

Tree: large tree, single straight trunk with a flared base (buttress), few low branches, many short branches clustering near crown

Leaf: simple, obovate, 5–8" (13–20 cm) long, alternately attached, few irregular teeth, thick, shiny green above, paler below and sometimes with hairs near the midrib, on a long hairy leafstalk

Bark: dark brown to reddish brown, smooth, becoming furrowed with scaly ridges with age

Fruit: green berry-like fruit (drupe), turning dark purple at maturity, thin sour pulp, oblong, 1" (2.5 cm) long, containing 1 seed

Fall Color: yellow

Origin/Age: native; 100–150 years

Habitat: wet soils, swamps, floodplains, in standing water, partial shade to sun

Range: far eastern edge of Texas in about 10–12 counties

Stan's Notes: This is an aquatic tree, hence its common name. Not uncommon for it to grow where standing water covers its roots for several months. The buttress helps to stabilize and hold the tree upright in water-saturated soil. The genus *Nyssa* is a Greek name referring to Greek water nymphs, or goddesses of lakes and rivers. Also called Swamp Tupelo, Cottongum, Watergum or Sourgum, the latter being another common name for Black Tupelo (pg. 239). Its tall straight trunk provides good lumber for furniture and building projects. Fruit matures in early fall and is eaten by wildlife such as bears, raccoons, ducks, turkeys and other birds.

bark

flower

fruit

Sweetbay
Magnolia virginiana

SIMPLE
ALTERNATE

Family: Magnolia (Magnoliaceae)

Height: 20–40' (6.1–12.2 m)

Tree: small to medium tree, many thin trunks from a central base, narrow pointed crown

Leaf: simple, oblong, 3–6" (7.5–15 cm) long, alternately attached, with a smooth edge (margin), slightly thick, shiny green above, paler with white-to-silver hairs below, on a short leafstalk

Bark: gray, smooth

Flower: cup-shaped creamy white flower, 2–3" (5–7.5 cm) wide, composed of 9–12 petals, solitary at the end of branch, lemony fragrance

Fruit: smooth green aggregate, turning red at maturity, cone-shaped, 1–2" (2.5–5 cm) long, splitting open in autumn and releasing many bright red seeds

Fall Color: semi-evergreen

Origin/Age: native; 50–100 years

Habitat: wet soils, along coastal wetlands, rivers, streams, sun to partial shade

Range: eastern edge of Texas, planted in parks and yards

Stan's Notes: A much loved magnolia tree with fragrant leaves and intensely lemon-scented flowers. Flowers start to bloom in mid-June and continue blooming into summer. The cone-shaped fruit is smooth, not like the fuzzy fruit of other magnolias. Fruit opens in autumn and releases many bright red seeds. "Bay" in the common name comes from early botanists, who used the term to refer to all evergreen and semi-evergreen trees with broad leaves. Also known as Sweetbay Magnolia or Swamp Magnolia.

bark

flower

fruit

Southern Magnolia
Magnolia grandiflora

Family: Magnolia (Magnoliaceae)

Height: 60–80' (18–24 m)

Tree: medium to large tree, single straight trunk, large conical crown

Leaf: simple, elliptical, 5–10" (13–25 cm) long, alternately attached, toothless margin, thick, leathery, shiny green above, paler with rusty hairs below

Bark: medium to dark gray, smooth when young, large scaly patches with age

Flower: large cup-shaped white flower, 6–10" (15–25 cm) wide, solitary at the end of branch, very fragrant

Fruit: large green aggregate, turning red when mature, cone-shaped, 3–6" (7.5–15 cm) long, covered with woolly hairs, splitting open in autumn, releasing seeds that hang on slender silken threads

Fall Color: semi-evergreen

Origin/Age: native; 50–100 years

Habitat: moist soils, deciduous forests, sun to partial shade

Range: eastern edge of Texas, Pineywoods, planted in parks and yards

Stan's Notes: A favorite tree to plant as an ornamental because of its large fragrant flowers or for shade. Several cultivated varieties now exist, with hardy varieties planted as far north as New York. Each flower opens by midmorning and closes at night. Blossoms last only a few days. Flowers from April through June. Fruit ripens during September and October, releasing many seeds after splitting open. Each seed hangs temporarily from a thin silken thread before falling to the ground. Also known as Evergreen Magnolia, Bullbay or Largeflower Magnolia.

bark

fruit

Chalk Maple
Acer leucoderme

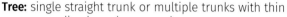

Family: Maple (Aceraceae)

Height: 10–20' (3–6.1 m)

Tree: single straight trunk or multiple trunks with thin ascending branches, round crown

Leaf: lobed, 2–3½" (5–9 cm) long, oppositely attached, 3 large lobes, drooping with pointed tips, deep notches and double-toothed margin, yellow green above, bright green and hairy below

Bark: pale gray to white, thin and chalky, becoming dark brown and furrowed at the tree base with age

Flower: tiny yellow flower, ⅛" (.3 cm) long, dangling on a stalk, 1–2" (2.5–5 cm) long

Fruit: pair of green winged seeds (samara), turning brown, ½–1" (1–2.5 cm) long

Fall Color: red to orange

Origin/Age: native; 100–125 years

Habitat: wet soils, moist soils, along streams and rivers, partial sun

Range: isolated in 3–4 counties in far eastern Texas

Stan's Notes: Certainly the most uncommon maple tree in Texas. Not confirmed in Texas until 1977, when it was located in Jasper and Sabine Counties and subsequently found in San Augustine and Newton Counties. Most common in Sabine National Forest. Unique chalky white bark gives it the common name and makes the species easy to identify. The leaves droop and leaf undersides have fine hairs that feel like velvet. The tree flowers in March and April, with fruit maturing in May and June. Wildlife eat the seeds.

bark

fruit

Southern Sugar Maple
Acer barbatum

Family: Maple (Aceraceae)

Height: 40–60' (12.2–18 m)

Tree: single straight trunk, many ascending branches, narrow pointed crown

Leaf: lobed, 2–3½" (5–9 cm) long, oppositely attached, 3–5 short lobes, smooth margin or with a few coarse teeth, dark green above, paler with fine hairs below

Bark: light gray to white, smooth, becoming furrowed with age

Fruit: pair of green winged seeds (samara), turning tan, ¾–2" (2–5 cm) long

Fall Color: yellow and red

Origin/Age: native; 100–150 years

Habitat: rich moist soils in a wide variety of habitats, along streams and rivers, valleys, sun

Range: far eastern edge of Texas

Stan's Notes: Closely related to the Sugar Maple (*A. saccharum*), (not shown), which does not occur in Texas. Hybridizes with Sugar Maple elsewhere where their ranges overlap. For many years it was thought that the Southern Sugar Maple was a subspecies or variety of Sugar Maple, with smaller leaves. Southern Sugar Maple can be tapped to gather sap for making maple syrup, but it is reported to have significantly less flow than Sugar Maple. In Texas most grow to only 40 feet (12.2 m) tall. Depending on the habitat, some have reached nearly 100 feet (30 m). Also called Florida Maple.

bark

flower

fruit

Red Maple
Acer rubrum

Family: Maple (Aceraceae)

Height: 40–60' (12.2–18 m)

Tree: single or multiple trunks, branching close to the ground, narrow dense crown

Leaf: lobed, 3–4" (7.5–10 cm) long, oppositely attached, 3–5 lobes (usually 3), shallow notches in between lobes, double-toothed margin, light green color, leafstalk red

Bark: gray, smooth, broken by narrow irregular cracks

Flower: tiny red hanging flower, ¼" (.6 cm) wide, on a 1–2" (2.5–5 cm) long red stalk, growing in clusters, 1–3" (2.5–7.5 cm) wide

Fruit: pair of winged seeds (samara), red in springtime, ½–1" (1–2.5 cm) long

Fall Color: red to orange

Origin/Age: native; 75–100 years

Habitat: wet to moist soils, along swamps or depressions that hold water, sun to partial shade

Range: eastern edge of Texas, Pineywoods, Gulf Prairies

Stan's Notes: One of the most drought-tolerant species of maple in Texas. Often planted as an ornamental tree, it can be identified by its characteristic leaves, which have three pointed lobes, and the red leafstalks. Common name comes from the obvious red flowers that bloom early in spring, but the flowers and leafstalks are not the only part of the tree that has red colors. New leaves, fall color and spring seeds are also red. Produces one of the smallest seeds of any of the maples. Also known as Drummond Red Maple, Trident Red Maple, Swamp Maple or Water Maple. Sometimes called Soft Maple even though this does not describe its very hard and brittle wood.

bark

fruit

Bigtooth Maple
Acer grandidentatum

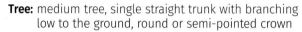

Family: Maple (Aceraceae)

Height: 30–50' (9.1–15 m)

Tree: medium tree, single straight trunk with branching low to the ground, round or semi-pointed crown

Leaf: lobed, 2–5" (5–13 cm) long, oppositely attached, 3–5 lobes (usually 3), rounded tips, large irregular teeth, wavy margin, dark green above, paler below

Bark: brown and thin when young, becoming narrowly furrowed with irregular ridges with age

Flower: greenish yellow flower, ¼" (.6 cm) wide, dangling on a 1–2" (2.5–5 cm) long stalk

Fruit: pair of green winged seeds (samara), turning tan, ¾–1½" (2–4 cm) long

Fall Color: red to orange, sometimes yellow

Origin/Age: native; 150–200 years

Habitat: moist soils, along streams and rivers, wet canyons, sun to partial shade

Range: scattered locations throughout central and western Texas, planted in parks and yards

Stan's Notes: A native maple of the western half of America from Idaho south to Arizona and east to central Texas. Grows in sheltered canyons in low to medium elevations with a consistent supply of water. Often planted as an ornamental tree for its shade and autumn color. The species name *grandidentatum*, Latin for "large tooth," describes the leaves. Can be tapped to collect sap for syrup when growing in locations that have cold temperatures at night. Also called Sabinal Maple, Rocky Mountain Sugar Maple and Western Sugar Maple. It has one subspecies, usually called Canyon Maple.

bark

flower

fruit

Sassafras

Sassafras albidum

Family: Laurel (Lauraceae)

Height: 30–60' (9.1–18 m)

Tree: medium-size columnar tree with a single crooked trunk, branches often crooked and spreading, flat irregular crown

Leaf: lobed or simple, 3–5" (7.5–13 cm) long, alternately attached, often has 1, 2 or 3 lobes with mitten-shaped 1–lobed leaves, simple elliptical leaves along with lobed leaves appear on the same tree, smooth toothless margin, shiny green above, paler below and often hairy

Bark: brown, deeply furrowed with age

Flower: green-to-yellow flower, ¼" (.6 cm) wide, on a 1–2" (2.5–5 cm) long stalk, in clusters

Fruit: blue-to-black fruit (drupe), ½" (1 cm) wide, on a 1" (2.5 cm) long fruit stalk, in clusters, containing 1 seed

Fall Color: yellow to red

Origin/Age: native; 100–150 years

Habitat: sandy soils, forest edges, sun to partial sun

Range: far eastern Texas, Pineywoods, Post Oak Savannah

Stan's Notes: "Sassafras" is an American Indian name. Like other Laurels, its crushed leaves and twigs have a spicy fragrance. It has soft wood, which breaks easily. Roots are shallow and once supplied oil of sassafras for perfumed soap. Settlers brewed its bark and roots into a tea for supposed medicinal purposes. One of our first exports. Produces dense cover and fruit for wildlife. Sometimes planted as an ornamental for its fall colors and fruit.

flower

bark

immature fruit

fruit

Sweetgum
Liquidambar styraciflua

Family: Witch-hazel (Hamamelidaceae)

Height: 80–100' (24–30 m)

Tree: tall tree, single straight trunk, wide at the bottom, narrow at the top, pointed crown

Leaf: lobed, star-shaped, 3–6" (7.5–15 cm) long, alternately attached, 5–7 long pointed lobes, fine teeth, 5 main veins from the notched base to lobe tips, shiny dark green above, whitish green below

Bark: gray to brown, deeply furrowed into narrow scales

Flower: ball-shaped green flower, ½–¾" (1–2 cm) wide, in clusters on a drooping stalk, 1–2" (2.5–5 cm) long

Fruit: round green cluster, turning brown at maturity, 1–1½" (2.5–4 cm) diameter, with many hard woody spines on a long fruit stalk, many flat winged seeds

Fall Color: red, sometimes orange or yellow

Origin/Age: native; 100–150 years

Habitat: moist and dry soils, river valleys, woods, uplands

Range: eastern edge of Texas, Pineywoods, Gulf Prairies, Post Oak Savannah

Stan's Notes: Often planted as a shade tree and for its bright red leaves in fall. Can be in pure stands, but usually grows with other deciduous trees. Moderately rapid growing. Matures at 20–25 years. Flowers in spring. Fruit matures in fall and opens to release seeds. Seeds eaten by birds and animals. Old fruit may stay on the tree in winter. An important tree commercially, surpassed only by oaks. Hard, heavy, dark reddish brown wood is used for furniture veneer, plywood and barrels. Well known for its resin, which is scraped off peeled bark. The gum has been used in adhesives, medicinally in soaps and for chewing gum. Leaves are aromatic when crushed.

bark

Bigelow Oak
Quercus sinuate breviloba

Family: Beech (Fagaceae)

Height: 10–20' (3–6.1 m)

Tree: small shrubby tree with many smaller trunks or a single trunk tree, open wide crown

Leaf: lobed, oblong, 1–3" (2.5–7.5 cm) long, alternately attached, with several round lobes, each broadest at the tip, thick and leathery, no teeth, light green above, pale below

Bark: gray, thin and smooth when young, becoming pale gray and very shaggy with age

Fruit: green acorn, turning brown at maturity, oblong, ¾" (2 cm) long, on a short stalk, shallow cap covering upper third of nut, often in clusters or pairs, maturing in 1 season

Fall Color: red to brown

Origin/Age: native; 200–250 years

Habitat: limestone soils, prairies, old fields, pastures, rolling hills, grasslands, sun

Range: central and northeastern Texas

Stan's Notes: Many hybrids of this species occur, with the *breviloba* variety being the most common in Texas. Usually a multi-trunk tree of grasslands, prairies and such. Almost always seen growing in limestone soils, spreading out low over the ground to form a thicket. Often known as Scrub Oak or Shin Oak since it generally reaches only 10 feet (3 m) tall and looks like a shrub. On rare occasions it grows as a single tree and can reach upwards of 30 feet (9.1 m). As it ages the bark turns pale gray and becomes shaggy, making the tree easier to identify. A white oak, very similar to Lacey Oak (pg. 155), but the unique bark of the Bigelow helps to differentiate.

bark

fruit

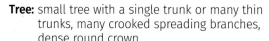

Sand Post Oak
Quercus margaretta

Family: Beech (Fagaceae)

Height: 10–20' (3–6.1 m)

Tree: small tree with a single trunk or many thin trunks, many crooked spreading branches, dense round crown

Leaf: lobed, 2–5" (5–13 cm) long, alternately attached, with 3–5 broad lobes, each with a round tip, waxy, leathery, shiny green above, dull green and hairy below

Bark: gray, deeply furrowed into long narrow strips

Fruit: green acorn, turning brown when mature, edible, nearly round, ½–¾" (1–2 cm) long, with a stout pointed tip, single or in pairs on a very short stalk, cap covers upper half of nut, maturing in 1 season

Fall Color: brown to yellow

Origin/Age: native; 250–400 years

Habitat: dry sandy soils, pine forests, sun

Range: scattered and isolated in eastern and central Texas, Pineywoods, Post Oak Savanna

Stan's Notes: Strong association with pure sand soils. Tolerates dry, sandy or gravelly soils where few other forest oaks live. Often forms thickets, usually directly associated with the size and shape of the sand deposit in the soil. Forms thickets by suckering roots, which send up genetically identical sprouts. Distinguished from other post oaks by having smaller leaves with more variable lobes and hairless twigs. A white oak group member. Acorns mature in one season and are eaten by many species of wildlife. Also called Dwarf Post Oak, Scrubby Post Oak, Post Oak and Runner Oak.

bark

fruit

Texas Red Oak
Quercus buckleyi

LOBED ALTERNATE

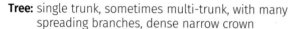

Family: Beech (Fagaceae)

Height: 30–50' (9.1–15 m)

Tree: single trunk, sometimes multi-trunk, with many spreading branches, dense narrow crown

Leaf: lobed, 3–4" (7.5–10 cm) long, alternately attached, deeply divided with 5–9 narrow pointed lobes, each narrowest in the middle, with 1 or more pointed tips, leathery, shiny light green above, dull green and slightly hairy below

Bark: dark gray with many plate-like scales

Fruit: green acorn, turning reddish brown at maturity, oval, 1" (2.5 cm) long, single or in pairs on a very short stalk, cap covering the upper third of nut, maturing in 2 seasons

Fall Color: red and orange

Origin/Age: native; 250–400 years

Habitat: sandy and alkaline clay soils, limestone ridges, slopes, occasionally along rivers and streams, sun

Range: north central and central Texas except for the panhandle, west to the Pecos River

Stan's Notes: A medium-size, very confusing oak tree that, in the past, has been identified as a different species. It hybrids with other oak species, producing trees with characteristics of both parents. Leaves appear very similar to the leaves of Nuttall Oak (pg. 269), but their ranges don't overlap. More drought tolerant than Shumard Oak (pg. 275), but less hardy. Susceptible to oak wilt. Produces large numbers of acorns that are eaten by wildlife despite the high tannin, which makes them not especially palatable. Species name is for Samuel B. Buckley, a botanist and geologist of Texas.

bark

fruit

Blackjack Oak
Quercus marilandica

Family: Beech (Fagaceae)

Height: 25–40' (7.6–12.2 m)

Tree: small to medium tree, single straight trunk, many crooked spreading branches, wide irregular crown

Leaf: lobed, club-shaped, 2–6" (5–15 cm) long, alternately attached, shallowly divided with 3–5 broad lobes, each broadest at the top, bristle-tipped, leathery, waxy, shiny dark green above, dull green below with brown hairs along veins

Bark: nearly black bark that is rough, thick and deeply furrowed into nearly square plates

Fruit: green acorn, turning brown when mature, edible, oblong, ½–¾" (1–2 cm) long, with a stout pointed tip, single or in pairs on a very short stalk, cap covers the upper half of nut, matures in 2 seasons

Fall Color: brown to yellow

Origin/Age: native; 150–200 years

Habitat: dry, sandy or clay soils, often on upland ridges, sun

Range: eastern half of Texas except the far south

Stan's Notes: One of the most widespread of oaks in Texas. Often associated with poor sandy soils. Tolerates dry, sandy or gravelly soils where few other forest oaks live. Also called Scrub Oak due to its stunted, scrubby growth. First described in the early 1700s by a colony in Maryland, hence the species name. Club-shaped leaves give it the common name. Leaves are covered with a waxy substance (cutin) that helps reduce water loss in hot, dry environments. Retains leaves well into winter. A black (red) oak, with small acorns taking two years to mature. New shoots sprout from burned or cut trunks. Wood is sometimes used for railroad ties and firewood.

bark

Chisos Red Oak
Quercus gravesii

Family: Beech (Fagaceae)

Height: 10–30' (3–9.1 m)

Tree: small oak with a single trunk, spreading branches, dense broad crown

Leaf: lobed, 3–5" (75–13 cm) long, alternately attached, with 3–7 broadly pointed lobes, each narrowest at the tip, with a pointed tip, leathery, shiny light green above, dull green below

Bark: reddish gray with many thin flat-topped scales

Fruit: green acorn, turning brown when mature, oval, 1" (2.5 cm) long, single or in pairs on a very short stalk, cap covering the upper third to half of nut, maturing in 2 seasons

Fall Color: red and orange

Origin/Age: native; 100–250 years

Habitat: sandy soils usually above 5,000' (1,525 m), limestone ridges, slopes

Range: high country of the Chisos, Davis, Del Norte and Glass Mountains, west of the Pecos River

Stan's Notes: A small oak that can be common in some canyons of the Chisos Mountains, hence its common name. Discovered in the 1850s, but was not rediscovered until the mid-1900s. One of the best places to see it is in the Basin of the Chisos in late fall (November and December), when the leaves turn bright colors. The only oak west of the Trans-Pecos that turns red in fall. Not much is known about the species, but it appears to be very drought tolerant and could be good to plant in parks and yards. Grown as far north as Dallas, but in this area it just drops its leaves in autumn without changing color. Closely related to Texas Red Oak (pg. 263) and Shumard Oak (pg. 275).

bark

fruit

Nuttall Oak
Quercus texana

Family: Beech (Fagaceae)

Height: 60–80' (18–24 m)

Tree: medium to large tree with a single straight trunk and broad, open round crown composed of many horizontal and drooping branches

Leaf: lobed, elliptical, 3–6" (7.5–15 cm) long, alternately attached, 5–7 long pointed lobes, each ending in a sharp tip (bristle-tipped), with wide deep sinuses in between lobes, dark green above, paler below with tufts of hair along the midrib

Bark: gray and smooth, becoming brown and furrowed with scaly ridges with age

Fruit: green acorn, turning brown and often with dark stripes at maturity, edible, oblong, ¾–1¼" (2–3 cm) long, cap covering the upper quarter to half of nut, maturing in 2 seasons

Fall Color: red to orange, turning brown

Origin/Age: native; 100–150 years

Habitat: wet or clay soils, often in river floodplains, full sun

Range: extreme southeastern corner of Texas, planted in parks and yards

Stan's Notes: Known for its red-orange fall foliage. Leaf shape is like Shumard Oak (pg. 275). Fairly disease resistant, it is planted along streets and boulevards and does well in urban environments. Does not do well in chalky, calcareous soils around Austin, Dallas and San Antonio. First described in 1927 and named Q. nuttallii for British-American botanist and ornithologist Thomas Nuttall (1786–1859). Sometimes called Texas Red Oak. Grows across Louisiana, Arkansas, Missouri, Mississippi and Alabama, but never in large numbers.

269

bark

flower

fruit

Gambel Oak
Quercus gambelii

Family: Beech (Fagaceae)

Height: 25–30' (7.6–9.1 m)

Tree: single or multiple short trunks, branching close to the ground, dense broad round crown

Leaf: lobed, 3–6½" (7.5–16 cm) long, alternately attached, 5–9 rounded lobes, deeply cut sinuses, often widest above the middle, no teeth, yellowish green above, paler and sometimes with hairs below

Bark: light gray, sometimes whitish, thin and smooth, becoming rough and breaking in furrows with age

Flower: green catkin, 1–1¼" (2.5–3 cm) long, composed of many tiny flowers, ⅛" (.3 cm) wide

Fruit: green acorn, turning brown at maturity, edible, ovate, ½–1½" (1–4 cm) long, solitary or in small clusters, short stalk or stalkless, cap covering the upper third of nut, maturing in 1 season

Fall Color: yellow to red brown

Origin/Age: native; 150–250 years

Habitat: rocky soils above 7,000' (2,135 m), canyons, hillsides, sun

Range: scattered in the Chinati, Chisos, Guadalupe and Davis Mountains in the Trans-Pecos region

Stan's Notes: Not common even in habitats where it does best. In Texas it never grows at low elevations in the wild. Grows slowly. Seen singly in the open; also forms dense thickets. Wildlife depend on it for food. Flowers of both sexes occur on the same tree (monoecious). Named for William Gambel, a nineteenth century plant collector and assistant curator of the National Academy of Sciences. Also called Rocky Mountain White Oak, Utah White Oak or Scrub Oak.

bark

fruit

Post Oak
Quercus stellata

Family: Beech (Fagaceae)

Height: 25–60' (7.6–18 m)

Tree: stout medium-size tree with a straight trunk and wide spreading branches, round crown

Leaf: lobed, unique shape suggests a Maltese cross, 3–7" (7.5–18 cm) long, alternately attached, 5–7 deep, squared lobes with 2 large middle lobes, rounded tip, tapered base, dark green above, paler below, leafstalk often stout and hairy, yellow star-shaped hairs on underside of leaf

Bark: light gray with scaly ridges

Fruit: green acorn, turning brown when mature, edible, egg-shaped (ovate), ½–1" (1–2.5 cm) long, single on a very short stalk or stalkless, thin cap covering the upper third of nut, maturing in 1 season

Fall Color: brown

Origin/Age: native; 200–250 years

Habitat: sandy gravelly soils, dry rocky soils, hills, ridges, along streams and rivers in floodplains, sun

Range: eastern two-thirds of Texas, planted in poor soils

Stan's Notes: By far the most wide-ranging oak in Texas. Some can reach upwards of 80 feet (24 m), but most are scrubby, only 25 feet (7.6 m) tall. Slow growing and drought resistant, planted in poor dry soils where other oaks won't survive. Unique leaf shape makes it easy to identify, but shape varies. Some leaves look like a cross. Thick yellowish twigs and star-shaped hairs on leaves help identify. *Stellata* refers to the shape of hairs. Wood was used for fence posts, hence the common name. Produces acorns each year, but has heavy crops every 2–4 years. An important food source for wildlife.

bark

fruit

Shumard Oak
Quercus shumardii

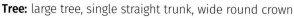

Family: Beech (Fagaceae)

Height: 60–90' (18–27 m)

Tree: large tree, single straight trunk, wide round crown

Leaf: lobed, 3–7" (7.5–18 cm) long, alternately attached, 5–9 pointed lobes, round sinuses, deeply divided nearly to the midrib, broadest at the top, several bristle-tipped teeth, dark green above, dull green below with tufts of hair at vein angles

Bark: gray, becoming darker with age, shallow furrows

Fruit: green acorn, turning brown when mature, edible, egg-shaped (ovate), ¾–1¼" (2–3 cm) long, single or in pairs on a short stalk, cap covering the upper third to half of nut, maturing in 2 seasons

Fall Color: red to brown

Origin/Age: native; 150–200 years

Habitat: moist soils, along rivers, streams and swamps

Range: eastern third of Texas except the far south

Stan's Notes: One of the largest oaks in Texas, some growing to nearly 100 feet (30), with a very wide crown. Grows the best in well-drained soils along rivers. Considered an oak of southern states, where it is planted as an ornamental tree. Hybridizes with other oak species, especially Texas Red Oak (pg. 263), making them hard to distinguish. A moderately fast-growing tree that flowers in spring. Acorns mature in the fall of their second year, with very large acorn crops occurring every 4–6 years. Susceptible to oak wilt. Wood has been used for flooring, veneers and furniture. Member of the black (red) oak group and sold as Red Oak. Named for B. F. Shumard, state geologist of Texas in the mid-1800s.

fruit

bark

flower

White Oak
Quercus alba

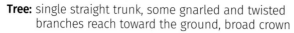

Family: Beech (Fagaceae)

Height: 50–70' (15–21 m)

Tree: single straight trunk, some gnarled and twisted branches reach toward the ground, broad crown

Leaf: lobed, 4–8" (10–20 cm) long, alternately attached, 5–9 rounded lobes, notches deeply cut or shallow and uniform in size and depth, often widest above the middle, lacking teeth, bright green above, paler below, leaves often clustered at ends of branches

Bark: light gray or light tan, broken into reddish scales

Flower: green catkin, 1–3" (2.5–7.5 cm) long, composed of many tiny flowers, ⅛" (.3 cm) wide

Fruit: green acorn, turning brown at maturity, edible, ½–1½" (1–4 cm) long, cap covering upper third of nut, maturing in 1 season

Fall Color: red brown

Origin/Age: native; 150–250 years

Habitat: variety of soil types including deep, well-drained, sand and clay, sun

Range: far eastern Texas, Pineywoods, Gulf Prairies

Stan's Notes: Usually occurs by itself and is almost never in large stands. Important in the lumber industry (but not in Texas), used for furniture, flooring, whiskey barrels, crates and much more. A white oak group member. Produces edible acorns each fall, with large crops occurring every 4–10 years. Like other acorns, these should be boiled before eating in several changes of water to leech out the bitter and slightly toxic tannin. Acorns are an important food source for turkeys, squirrels, grouse, deer and other wildlife. Susceptible to oak wilt.

bark

fruit

Black Oak

Quercus velutina

LOBED ALTERNATE

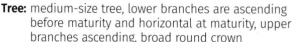

Family: Beech (Fagaceae)

Height: 40–60' (12.2–18 m)

Tree: medium-size tree, lower branches are ascending before maturity and horizontal at maturity, upper branches ascending, broad round crown

Leaf: lobed, 4–9" (10–23 cm) long, alternately attached, 5–7 lobes, each ending in a pointed tip (bristle-tipped) and separated by deep U-shaped sinuses, shiny green above, yellowish brown below

Bark: shiny dark gray and smooth texture when young, becoming nearly black with deep reddish cracks

Flower: light yellow catkin, 1–3" (2.5–7.5 cm) long, made up of many tiny flowers, ⅛" (.3 cm) wide

Fruit: green acorn, turning brown at maturity, ¾" (2 cm) long, almost as wide as long, thin black vertical lines on hull, cap covering the upper half of nut

Fall Color: orange brown

Origin/Age: native; 175–200 years

Habitat: dry sandy soils, gravelly soils, slopes, ridges, sun

Range: eastern edge of Texas, Pineywoods

Stan's Notes: Uncommon in Texas. Grows singly or in pairs, never in pure stands. Two oak groups, red (sometimes called black) and white, with the Black Oak a member of the red (black) oak group. Acorns of the red (black) oak group mature in two seasons, while white oak group acorns mature in one season. Produces heavy fruit crops only infrequently. Nuts are bitter due to tannic acid (tannin). Bark also contains tannin, which was used in tanning animal skins. New leaves unfurling in spring are crimson before turning silvery, then dark green. Highly susceptible to oak wilt disease.

bark

fruit

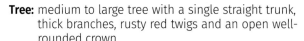
Southern Red Oak
Quercus falcata

Family: Beech (Fagaceae)

Height: 60–80' (18–24 m)

Tree: medium to large tree with a single straight trunk, thick branches, rusty red twigs and an open well-rounded crown

Leaf: lobed, 5–9" (13–23 cm) long, alternately attached, 3–5 (usually 3, sometimes up to 9) long narrow lobes, each with 1–3 pointed tips (bristle-tipped), deep sinuses, shiny green above, lighter below with rust or gray hairs

Bark: dark gray to brown, many broad ridges and plates

Fruit: green acorn, turning brown when mature, edible, oblong or round, ½–¾" (1–2 cm) long, on a short stalk, red brown cap covering the upper third of nut, maturing in 2 seasons

Fall Color: brown

Origin/Age: native; 100–150 years

Habitat: dry sandy soils, upland in mixed forests, sun to partial shade

Range: upper eastern edge of Texas, Pineywoods, Gulf Prairies and Marshes

Stan's Notes: Can be the most common oak in the Pineywoods. As its common name implies, this tree grows mainly in the southern states from Florida to southern New York and west to Texas. A fast-growing species that provides shade. Leaves can be highly variable, but they usually have three lobes. Regardless of the number, lobes are always bristle-tipped. Lumber is used for flooring and furniture. Sometimes called Spanish Oak. Also known as Swamp Red Oak, Swamp Spanish Oak, Cherrybark Oak or Bottomland Red Oak.

bark

fruit

Overcup Oak
Quercus lyrata

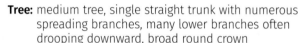

Family: Beech (Fagaceae)

Height: 40–60' (12.2–18 m)

Tree: medium tree, single straight trunk with numerous spreading branches, many lower branches often drooping downward, broad round crown

Leaf: lobed, 5–10" (13–25 cm) long, alternately attached, 5–9 rounded lobes, no teeth, dark green above, paler below and often with scattered whitish hairs

Bark: light gray to brown, thick with scaly furrows

Fruit: green acorn, turning brown when mature, edible, ½–1" (1–2.5 cm) long, thin scaly cap nearly covering the nut, maturing in 1 season

Fall Color: yellow or red, turning brown

Origin/Age: native; 150–200 years

Habitat: wide variety of poor soils including wet clay, floodplains, along swamps and other wet areas, sun or partial shade

Range: eastern edge of Texas, Pineywoods, Gulf Prairies and Marshes

Stan's Notes: Almost always growing in wet conditions. Also called Swamp Post Oak or Swamp White Oak due to its preferred habitat of wet soils. Very tolerant of flooding and can survive when roots are covered with standing water. A slow-growing, long-lived tree that may take up to 30 years before producing acorns. Acorns are edible and eaten by wildlife. Common name "Overcup" refers to the acorn cap, which nearly covers the nut. Latin species name *lyrata* means "lyre-shaped" and refers to the shape of the leaf, resembling the lyre instrument.

bark

flower

fruit

Bur Oak

Quercus macrocarpa

LOBED
ALTERNATE

Family: Beech (Fagaceae)

Height: 50–80' (15–24 m)

Tree: tall straight trunk, distinct nearly to top, branches and twigs thick, nearly horizontal lower branches, upper branches ascending, broad round crown

Leaf: lobed, 5–12" (13–30 cm) long, alternately attached, 7–9 rounded lobes, end (terminal) lobe often the largest, no teeth, shiny dark green, highly variable leaves cluster near the ends of twigs

Bark: dark gray, thick and corky, deeply furrowed with many ridges and scales

Flower: green catkin, 1–3" (2.5–7.5 cm) long, composed of many tiny flowers, ⅛" (.3 cm) wide

Fruit: green acorn, turning brown when mature, sweet and edible, 1–2" (2.5–5 cm) long, cap with hairy edge covering more than the upper half of nut

Fall Color: yellow or brown

Origin/Age: native; 150–250 years

Habitat: deep rich soils, sandy soils, shade tolerant

Range: northern Texas and eastern half except the eastern edge and far south, planted in yards and parks

Stan's Notes: One of the easiest oaks to grow. Drought tolerant, making it a fine choice for yards and parks. Thick bark allows it to withstand fires. White oak group member (rounded lobes; ripe nuts in one season). Leaves vary, but lobes are always rounded, with the end lobe the largest. Latin species name *macro* ("large") and *carpa* ("finger") refer to the end lobe. Heavy nut crop every 3–5 years. Most acorns have Nut Weevil larvae. Often has oak gall, a fleshy deformity caused by wasp larvae. Also called Blue Oak or Mossycup Oak.

bark

Baretta
Helietta parvifolia

Family: Rue (Rutaceae)

Height: 15–20' (4.6–6.1 m)

Tree: small slender tree with many short trunks divided close to the ground, broad irregular crown

Leaf: compound, spade-shaped, 1½–2" (4–5 cm) long, oppositely attached, made of 3 leaflets, each ½–2" (1–5 cm) long, widest near or above the middle, with a round or pointed tip (sometimes notched), smooth edge, smooth and shiny yellowish green above, paler below, stalkless, strong pungent odor when crushed

Bark: gray to green, thin and smooth, breaking into large patches with age

Flower: greenish white flower, ⅜" (.9 cm) long, in clusters, 1–3" (2.5–7.5 cm) long, occurring at the junctions of upper leaves

Fruit: green winged fruit, turning yellow or tan when mature, ¼–½" (.6–1 cm) wide, in clusters of 3–4

Fall Color: evergreen

Origin/Age: native; 75–100 years

Habitat: sandy soils with good drainage, sun

Range: restricted to Starr County in Texas, planted in other counties in the far southern tip of the state

Stan's Notes: Before 1940, this small evergreen grew throughout the southern tip of Texas. Now grows only in parts of Starr County, but has been planted in the surrounding area. Widespread in Mexico, apparently reaching its northern limits in southern Texas. Flowers in March and April. Winged fruit ripens in September and October. Leaves are resinous, with an unpleasant aroma when crushed.

bark

fruit

Texas Pistache
Pistacia texana

Family: Sumac or Cashew (Anacardiaceae)

Height: 10–30' (3–9.1 m)

Tree: many thin trunks or a single straight trunk, with an irregular round crown

Leaf: compound, 4–6" (10–15 cm) long, oppositely attached, composed of 6–18 pairs of lance-shaped leaflets, each leaflet ½–1" (1–2.5 cm) long, with a pointed tip, smooth edge (margin), feathery, light green above, slightly lighter below

Bark: light gray, smooth

Fruit: small red, blue or purple berry (drupe), ⅛" (.4 cm) wide, in clusters

Fall Color: evergreen

Origin/Age: native; 100–150 years

Habitat: sandy soils, dry rocky soils, limestone cliffs, stream banks, sun

Range: isolated in Val Verde and Terrell Counties along the Rio Grande, Big Bend, planted in parks and yards

Stan's Notes: A small rare tree, once thought to be nearly extinct. It has been cultivated by the nursery trade and is now available for landscaping. Never occurs in great numbers and is found only in parts of Texas and scattered in Mexico. In most places it appears as a multi-trunk shrub. Grows thick enough to make a good fencerow. Provides good shelter and food for wildlife, growing quickly in dry soils and producing attractive colorful fruit.

fruit

bark

flower

Boxelder
Acer negundo

COMPOUND OPPOSITE

Family: Maple (Aceraceae)

Height: 30–50' (9.1–15 m)

Tree: medium-size tree, frequently with a divided and crooked trunk, broad irregular crown

Leaf: compound, 4–9" (10–23 cm) long, oppositely attached, composed of 3–5 leaflets, each leaflet 2–4" (5–10 cm) long, often 3-lobed, with irregular teeth, pale green

Bark: light gray to tan, becoming deeply furrowed with wavy ridges

Flower: tiny reddish flower, ¼" (.6 cm) wide, hanging in clusters on a stalk, 1–3" (2.5–7.5 cm) long

Fruit: pair of green winged seeds (samara), turning to brown at maturity, 1–2" (2.5–5 cm) long

Fall Color: yellow

Origin/Age: native; 50–60 years

Habitat: wet soils at 3,500–8,500' (1,065–2,590 m), along streams, lakes and flooded areas, sun

Range: eastern half of Texas except the far south

Stan's Notes: A fairly common tree in Texas. Unique species among native maple trees because its leaves are compound. A member of the Maple family with all the virtues, but none of the respect. Often considered a trash tree, but produces large amounts of seeds that stay on the tree in winter, making a valuable food source for wildlife. If the tree is tapped in spring, it yields sap that can be boiled into syrup. The sugar content is lower than in other maples, so it takes more sap to make a comparable syrup. Often covered with Boxelder Bugs, harmless beetles whose larvae eat the leaves but cause little damage. Also called Manitoba Maple or Ash-leaved Maple.

fruit

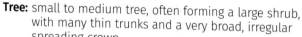

COMPOUND
OPPOSITE

Brazilian Peppertree
Schinus molle

Family: Sumac or Cashew (Anacardiaceae)

Height: 10–40' (3–12.2 m)

Tree: small to medium tree, often forming a large shrub, with many thin trunks and a very broad, irregular spreading crown

Leaf: compound, 6–10" (15–25 cm) long, oppositely attached, made up of 20–40 pairs of narrow lance-shaped leaflets, each leaflet ½–2" (1–5 cm) long, with a pointed tip, smooth margin, droopy and feathery, light green above, slightly lighter below

Bark: light gray, smooth

Flower: tiny cream-to-white flower, ¼" (.6 cm) wide, in large clusters, 6–8" (15–20 cm) long

Fruit: waxy pink-to-red berry (drupe), ¼" (.6 cm) wide, hanging in large clusters, resinous, with 1 seed

Fall Color: semi-evergreen

Origin/Age: non-native, introduced from South America; 100–125 years

Habitat: sandy rocky soils, old homesteads, along roads, sun

Range: planted in parks and yards, escaping into the wild

Stan's Notes: This is a graceful, attractive evergreen species that was imported from South America. Often forms a large shrub rather than the typical tree form. Sold as an ornamental tree and planted in parks and yards for many decades. Birds that have consumed the berries excreted the seeds in the wild, where they have taken root. Now flourishing in the wild. The entire plant is resinous, not just the berries. Oils in the leaves deter other plants from growing under its branches, resulting in bare ground at the base of the tree.

bark

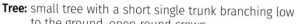
Mexican Ash
Fraxinus berlandieriana

Family: Olive (Oleaceae)

Height: 10–30' (3–9.1 m)

Tree: small tree with a short single trunk branching low to the ground, open round crown

Leaf: compound, 3–7" (7.5–18 cm) long, oppositely attached, composed of 3–5 lance-shaped leaflets, each leaflet 3–4" (7.5–10 cm) long, with shallow teeth or toothless margin, dark green and shiny above, paler below, on a leaflet stalk (petiolule), ¼" (.6 cm) long

Bark: gray and thick with many furrows and ridges

Fruit: green winged seed (samara), turning brown when mature, 1–1½" (2.5–4 cm) long, rounded wing tip

Fall Color: brown to light purple

Origin/Age: native; 100–150 years

Habitat: moist soils, around streams, rivers, moist canyons, wetlands, sun

Range: southern third of Texas, planted in yards, parks

Stan's Notes: Very similar to Green Ash (pg. 303), but has smaller compound leaves, fewer leaflets and slightly smaller fruit. Not very common in Texas, growing only in small pockets where there is enough moisture. Native to Texas and adjacent Mexico near any water source, especially in moist canyons. Blooms early in spring, with fruit following in May. Planted as a shade tree and ornamental because it seems more adapted to water and less humid climates.

bark

fruit

Gregg Ash
Fraxinus greggii

Family: Olive (Oleaceae)

Height: 10–20' (3–6.1 m)

Tree: shrub to small tree with several short trunks that often branch low to the ground, round crown

Leaf: compound, 3–7" (7.5–18 cm) long, oppositely attached, composed of 3–5 or 7 oblong leaflets, each leaflet ½–1" (1–2.5 cm) long, widest near the middle, toothless, leathery, light green and usually smooth

Bark: gray to nearly black and smooth when young, becoming furrowed with age

Fruit: pair of green winged seeds (samara), turning brown at maturity, ½–¾" (1–2 cm) long, with a rounded wing tip

Fall Color: yellow green

Origin/Age: native; 75–100 years

Habitat: dry rocky soils, hillsides, canyons, dry creek beds, along streams, sun

Range: southern edge of Texas along the border in the Trans-Pecos region, Big Bend

Stan's Notes: A shrub to small tree that occurs mainly in Mexico, reaching its northern limits in the canyons and dry rocky hillsides of the border country in the Trans-Pecos. It is most common in Blue Creek Canyon in Big Bend National Park. Flowers bloom in March and April; fruit follows in 9–12 weeks. Male and female flowers are found on separate trees (dioecious) or the same tree (monoecious). Leaves are eaten by many small and large mammals and seeds are eaten by many bird species. Reaches its largest size when growing along wet streams.

bark

fruit

Velvet Ash
Fraxinus velutina

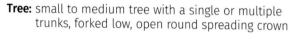

Family: Olive (Oleaceae)

Height: 30–50' (9.1–15 m)

Tree: small to medium tree with a single or multiple trunks, forked low, open round spreading crown

Leaf: compound, 4–6" (10–15 cm) long, oppositely attached, composed of 3–7 leaflets, each leaflet 1–1½" (2.5–4 cm) long, oval, broadest at the base, pointed tip, toothless edge or with a few teeth, pale green above, paler and velvety soft below

Bark: brown, thin and divided into shallow furrows and narrow scales

Fruit: green winged seed (samara), turning brown and papery at maturity, 1–1½" (2.5–4 cm) long, rounded wing tip, in clusters, staying on the tree into winter

Fall Color: yellow

Origin/Age: native; 50–100 years

Habitat: moist soils between 2,500–6,000' (760–1,830 m), along streams and washes, narrow canyons, sun to partial shade

Range: scattered in far western Texas, planted in parks and yards throughout

Stan's Notes: "Velvet" is for the densely packed soft hairs on the underside of leaves. The amount of velvet is highly variable. A good shade tree for Texas, planted in many parks and yards. Produces copious seeds, which are eaten by wildlife. Often grows with pines and cottonwoods, sometimes forming pure stands. Occurs in low to medium elevations from western Texas to southern New Mexico and Arizona, into southern Nevada and California. Also called Arizona Ash. Millions of these trees are dying due to insect borers.

bark

fruit

Texas Ash
Fraxinus texensis

Family: Olive (Oleaceae)

Height: 30–50' (9.1–15 m)

Tree: medium tree with a short trunk branching into many crooked branches, wide spreading crown

Leaf: compound, 4–8" (10–20 cm) long, oppositely attached, composed of 5 (rarely 7) nearly oval leaflets, each 1–3" (2.5–7.5 cm) long, widest before or near the middle, lacking teeth, leathery, dark green and usually smooth

Bark: dark gray, becoming deeply furrowed with age

Fruit: pair of green winged seeds (samara), turning brown at maturity, ¾–1" (2–2.5 cm) long, narrow with a rounded wing tip

Fall Color: red, orange and purple

Origin/Age: native; 75–100 years

Habitat: rocky soils, hillsides, limestone bluffs, full sun

Range: scattered in southern and central Texas, isolated pockets in north central Texas, planted in yards and parks

Stan's Notes: Closely related to the White Ash (pg. 307), but has smaller and fewer leaflets and smaller fruit. Grows only in Texas, with the exception of a few isolated pockets in Oklahoma. Found on limestone bluffs and cliffs in full sun. Male and female flowers are found on separate trees (dioecious) and bloom early in spring before the leaves appear, with fruit flowering about 10 weeks later. Highly drought tolerant, making it a great tree for landscapes due to its meager water requirement. It turns several beautiful shades of color in fall—another good reason to plant it around homes. Its light brown wood is strong, heavy and has been used in construction.

bark

fruit

Green Ash

Fraxinus pennsylvanica

Family: Olive (Oleaceae)

Height: 50–60' (15–18 m)

Tree: single straight trunk with ascending branches and irregular crown

Leaf: compound, 9–16" (23–40 cm) long, oppositely attached, made of 5–9 stalked leaflets, each leaflet 1–2" (2.5–5 cm) long, lacking teeth or with a very fine-toothed margin, on a very short leaflet stalk (petiolule), ⅛" (.3 cm) long

Bark: brown with deep furrows and narrow interlacing ridges, often appearing diamond-shaped

Fruit: green winged seed (samara), turning brown when mature, with a rounded end, sometimes notched, 1–2" (2.5–5 cm) long, in clusters, often remaining on the tree into winter

Fall Color: yellow

Origin/Age: native; 75–100 years

Habitat: wet soils, along streams, lowland forests, shade

Range: eastern half of Texas, scattered in the panhandle, planted in parks and yards

Stan's Notes: The most wide-ranging of the ash trees in Texas. Also known as Red Ash because it was once thought that Green Ash and Red Ash trees were separate species. These are now considered one species. Able to survive with its roots under water for several weeks early in spring. Often has a large unattractive growth (insect gall) at the ends of small branches that persists on the tree throughout the year. Its wood is strong and white and used to make baseball bats, tennis racquets, skis and snowshoes.

bark

flower

fruit

Carolina Ash
Fraxinus caroliniana

Family: Olive (Oleaceae)

Height: 20–40' (6.1–12.2 m)

Tree: single or multiple trunks, often leaning, enlarged base (buttress), narrow rounded crown

Leaf: compound, 5–12" (13–30 cm) long, oppositely attached, composed of 3–7 leaflets, each leaflet 2–4" (5–10 cm) long, coarse-toothed margin, green above, paler green to whitish and often slightly hairy below, on a thin long leaflet stalk (petiolule)

Bark: light gray, thin and scaly when young, becoming more scaly with age

Flower: green flower, ⅛" (.3 cm) wide, in loose clusters

Fruit: green winged (sometimes 3 wings) seed (samara), turning yellow to brown when mature, with large broad wings, 1¼–2" (3–5 cm) long, in clusters

Fall Color: yellow

Origin/Age: native; 40–70 years

Habitat: wet soils, along streams, rivers and swamps, shade to partial sun

Range: few counties in far eastern Texas near the coast

Stan's Notes: A small to medium tree of wet habitats. Also called Water Ash or Swamp Ash for its water-loving habitat. This is one of the smallest ash species in the eastern United States, with some of the largest winged seeds. Its large, broad winged seeds help identify the species. Male and female flowers bloom on separate trees (dioecious), resulting in just the female trees bearing seeds each season. Some say it is a commercially unimportant tree. Ranges from far eastern Texas to Florida and up the coast into the Carolinas.

fruit

bark

White Ash
Fraxinus americana

Family: Olive (Oleaceae)

Height: 40–60' (12.2–18 m)

Tree: medium-size tree with single straight trunk and narrow, open round crown

Leaf: compound, 8–12" (20–30 cm) long, oppositely attached, composed of 7 (occasionally 5–9) oval leaflets, each leaflet 3–5" (7.5–13 cm) long, with few teeth or toothless, dark green above, distinctly whiter in color below, on a leaflet stalk (petiolule), ¼–½" (.6–1 cm) long

Bark: greenish gray with many furrows and interlacing diamond-shaped ridges

Fruit: green winged seed (samara), turning brown when mature, 1–2" (2.5–5 cm) long, notched or rounded wing tip, remaining on the tree into winter

Fall Color: bronze purple

Origin/Age: native; 150–200 years

Habitat: deep, rich or well-drained soils, upland sites, sun

Range: eastern third of Texas

Stan's Notes: Very similar to the Green Ash (pg. 303), but tends to grow in sunny, dry, well-drained upland sites. Although it is the most abundant of all 16 ash tree species in the United States, it only occurs in part of Texas and is less common than Green Ash. Male and female flowers bloom on separate trees (dioecious) in April and May. Fast-growing, able to grow to 10 feet (3 m) in under 5 years. Produces seeds annually, with large amounts every 2–5 years. Young sprouts emerge from stumps or after fires. "White" refers to the pale underside of leaves. The straight narrow-grained wood is used for tennis racquets, baseball bats, snowshoes and hockey sticks.

thorn

bark

flower

fruit

Texas Palo Verde
Cercidium texanum

Family: Pea or Bean (Fabaceae)

Height: 15–25' (4.6–7.6 m)

Tree: many short, crooked green trunks branching near the ground, branches often zigzagging branchlets, leafless for part of the year, open irregular crown

Leaf: compound, 1–2" (2.5–5 cm) long, alternately attached, made of 2–6 tiny leaflets, each ¼" (.6 cm) long, feathery, dark green, leaflets often absent or fall off

Bark: green and smooth, becoming brown or red brown with age, pairs of straight thorns up to 1" (2.5 cm) long on green branches

Flower: 5–petaled, pea-like yellow flower, 1" (2.5 cm) wide, with red spots on the largest petal, in a cluster of 3–5 flowers

Fruit: pea-like green pod, turning tan with age, 1–2½" (2.5–6 cm) long, straight to curved with a pointed tip, containing 1–5 flattened, shiny dark seeds

Origin/Age: native; 50–100 years

Habitat: sandy soils, brushy plains, prairies, deserts, sun

Range: southern quarter of Texas, planted in the southern half of the state in parks and yards

Stan's Notes: This is an endemic species, with its unique range from northern Mexico reaching only into Texas. It has smaller leaves and shorter thorns than Mexican Palo Verde (pg. 311). The five-petaled yellow flowers bloom from March to November and are dependent on sufficient rainfall. Sometimes planted as a landscape shrub, doing well during drought years.

Mexican Palo Verde
Parkinsonia aculeata

Family: Pea or Bean (Fabaceae)

Height: 20–40' (6.1–12.2 m)

Tree: short crooked trunk or thinner multi-trunks that branch close to the ground, large arching branches, leafless for part of the year, open irregular crown

Leaf: compound, 5–12" (13–30 cm) long, alternately attached, made of 2 or 4 long, narrow, flattened, strap-like strips with 20–30 pairs of tiny leaflets, each ¼" (.6 cm) long, feathery, yellow green, leaflets often absent or fall off, leaving just the strap

Bark: green and smooth, becoming brown or red brown with age, pairs of straight thorns up to 2" (5 cm) long on green branches

Flower: 5–petaled, pea-like, orange-tinged yellow flower, 1–1½" (2.5–4 cm) wide, on an upright cluster made of 8–10 flowers, each cluster 5–6" (13–15 cm) tall

Fruit: pea-like green pod, turning tan with age, 2–4" (5–10 cm) long, straight to curved with a pointed tip

Origin/Age: native; 50–200 years

Habitat: moist or dry soils, at washes, rivers, canyons, sun

Range: southern edge of Texas along the Rio Grande from the Trans-Pecos region to the Gulf, planted in the southern half of the state in parks and yards

Stan's Notes: Excellent for landscaping in Texas due to its ability to survive severe droughts. When leaflets drop during a drought, photosynthesis occurs in the green central stalk (rachis) straps. The green branches and trunk are also photosynthetic and produce food for the tree when it is leafless. Also called Retama, Jerusalem Thorn or just Paloverde. Hybridizes with Texas Palo Verde (pg. 309).

thorn

bark

flower

fruit

Honey Mesquite
Prosopis glandulosa

Family: Pea or Bean (Fabaceae)

Height: 10–20' (3–6.1 m)

Tree: small tree with single or multiple short crooked trunks, branches arching and close to the ground, irregular crown

Leaf: compound, 1–2½" (2.5–6 cm) long, alternately attached, central stalk (rachis) splitting into 2 stalks, each with 10–20 pairs of narrow leaflets, each leaflet ½–¾" (1–2 cm) long, with a smooth edge and feathery appearance, bright green

Bark: brown and smooth, breaking up into long, narrow scaly strips with age, pairs of stout straight thorns on branches where leaves attach

Flower: green-to-yellow or white flower, ⅛" (.3 cm) long, in elongated clusters, 2–4" (5–10 cm) long

Fruit: large pea-like green pod, turning tan with age, 4–10" (10–25 cm) long, straight and rounded

Fall Color: yellow

Origin/Age: native; 50–100 years

Habitat: rocky and sandy soils, slopes, deserts, by streams, sun

Range: throughout Texas except the eastern edge

Stan's Notes: Distinguished from the other mesquites by its smooth-edged leaflets. Mesquite was an important, widespread resource for southwestern Indigenous peoples, providing food, fuel, shelter, weapons, tools, medicines, cosmetics, twist fibers, dyes and more. Its wood is legendary for cooking, smoking and curing meats. Range expanded when cattle ate the fruit and spread the seeds far and wide. Species name *glandulosa* refers to the nectar glands of the flower.

thorn

bark

flower

fruit

Screwbean Mesquite

Prosopis pubescens

COMPOUND ALTERNATE

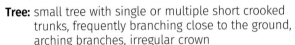

Family: Pea or Bean (Fabaceae)

Height: 10–25' (3–7.6 m)

Tree: small tree with single or multiple short crooked trunks, frequently branching close to the ground, arching branches, irregular crown

Leaf: compound, 1–2½" (2.5–6 cm) long, alternately attached, central stalk (rachis) splitting into 2 stalks, each with 10–20 pairs of narrow leaflets, each leaflet ½–¾" (1–2 cm) long, with a feathery appearance, slightly hairy, bright green

Bark: brown and smooth, breaking up into long, narrow scaly strips with age, pairs of stout straight thorns on branches where leaves attach

Flower: green-to-yellow or white flower, ⅛" (.3 cm) long, in elongated clusters, 2–4" (5–10 cm) long

Fruit: pea-like green pod, turning tan with age, edible, 1–2" (2.5–5 cm) long, tightly spiraled

Fall Color: yellow

Origin/Age: native; 50–100 years

Habitat: rocky and sandy soils, deserts, along streams, creeks and washes, sun

Range: scattered in the western edge of the Trans-Pecos

Stan's Notes: Distinguished from other mesquite trees by its hairy leaflets and fruit shape and size. Also called Screwpod Mesquite and Tornillo. Young pods are tender and sweet and have been cooked and eaten by many Indigenous peoples. Despite the stout thorns, deer and other large mammals browse the leaves and eat the seedpods. Like other mesquites, it can survive in desert conditions but thrives along washes and creeks where more water is available.

immature fruit

bark

flower

fruit

Texts Mountain Laurel

Sophora secundiflora

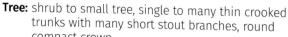

Family: Pea or Bean (Fabaceae)

Height: 10–25' (3–7.6 m)

Tree: shrub to small tree, single to many thin crooked trunks with many short stout branches, round compact crown

Leaf: compound, 4–6" (10–15 cm) long, alternately attached, composed of 5–9 spoon-shaped leaflets, each 1–1½" (2.5–4 cm) long, rounded (sometimes notched) tip, smooth margin, thick and leathery, shiny yellow green above, slightly lighter below

Bark: light gray with thin flat-topped scales

Flower: pea-shaped purple-to-lavender flower, ½–1" (1–2.5 cm) diameter, many hanging in large clusters, 4–7" (10–18 cm) long, strong grape-like fragrance

Fruit: large green pod, turning tan and woody when mature, round with 1 compartment or constricted between many compartments, with a pointed end, hanging in clusters, 1–5" (2.5–13 cm) long, containing large, poisonous red seeds

Fall Color: evergreen

Origin/Age: native; 100–125 years

Habitat: limestone soils, well-drained sandy soils, brushy slopes, sun

Range: southern half of Texas, planted in parks and yards

Stan's Notes: More often appears as a shrub with multiple trunks. Covered with stunning flowers that can be smelled from a distance. Blossoms face in one direction ("secund" inflorescence), hence the species name. Its evergreen leaves, fragrant flowers and interesting fruit make it a popular ornamental tree for parks and yards.

bark

flower

fruit

Eve's Necklace
Sophora affinis

Family: Pea or Bean (Fabaceae)

Height: 10–30' (3–9.1 m)

Tree: small tree with a single thin crooked trunk, many stout spreading branches, broad irregular crown

Leaf: compound, 6–9" (15–23 cm) long, alternately attached, composed of 9–15 oval leaflets, each leaflet ½–1½" (1–4 cm) long, with a pointed tip, smooth margin, droopy and feathery, yellow green and hairy above when young, lighter below and slightly hairy

Bark: light gray to brown, thin and scaly

Flower: 5–petaled, pea-shaped, small white-to-pink flower, ½" (1 cm) diameter, hanging in clusters, 2–5" (5–13 cm) long

Fruit: green pod, turning black when mature, leathery, slightly hairy, with a pointed end, hanging in clusters, 1–5" (2.5–13 cm) long, with 4–8 toxic seeds, constricted between seeds, appearing as separate beads on a string, pods stay on the tree in winter

Fall Color: yellow

Origin/Age: native; 100–125 years

Habitat: moist soils, along streams and other wet locations, along roads, sun

Range: central and eastern Texas excluding the panhandle

Stan's Notes: Named for its fruit, which looks like a string of beads or necklace that Eve might have worn. Seeds are poisonous, with pods remaining on the tree all winter. Often forms large thickets. Ranges from Texas into Oklahoma, Arkansas and Louisiana. Also called Texas Sophora, Pink Sophora or Necklacetree.

bark

flower

fruit

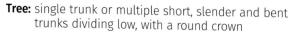

Prairie Sumac
Rhus lanceolata

Family: Sumac or Cashew (Anacardiaceae)

Height: 10–20' (3–6.1 m)

Tree: single trunk or multiple short, slender and bent trunks dividing low, with a round crown

Leaf: compound, 5–9" (13–23 cm) long, alternately attached, composed of 13–19 very narrow leaflets, each 1–2½" (2.5–6 cm) long and ½" (1 cm) wide, with a long pointed tip, sometimes curved, smooth margin, shiny dark green above, paler and hairy below, attaching directly to the central stalk (rachis)

Bark: gray to light brown and smooth, becoming scaly

Flower: pale green-to-yellow flower, ¼" (.6 cm) wide, in upright pyramidal clusters, 3–6" (7.5–15 cm) tall

Fruit: red berry-like fruit (drupe), ⅛" (.3 cm) diameter, covered with a dense coating of hairs, in cone-shaped clusters, 3–6" (7.5–15 cm) tall

Fall Color: reddish purple

Origin/Age: native; 25–50 years

Habitat: dry rocky or poor soils, forest edges, along highways, hillsides, valleys, sun

Range: central and western Texas, planted along roadways and in parks

Stan's Notes: A small tree to large shrub of central Texas, with a separate population in western Texas. Ranges from isolated patches in Oklahoma and New Mexico into portions of Texas and Mexico. Often forms thick patches or thickets, which attract wildlife for the dense protection. Many bird species feed on the fuzzy red berries. Deer and other large animals browse twigs and branches. The tree flowers in July and August, with fruit following in September.

bark

flower

fruit

Shining Sumac
Rhus copallina

Family: Sumac or Cashew (Anacardiaceae)

Height: 10–20' (3–6.1 m)

Tree: single or multiple trunks that are short, slender and often crooked or bent, round crown

Leaf: compound, 5–10" (13–25 cm) long, alternately attached, composed of 9–21 leaflets, each 1½–2½" (4–6 cm) long, smooth margin, smooth and dark green above, paler and hairy below, lacking a leaflet stalk (sessile), attaching directly to a central stalk (rachis) that is winged

Bark: light brown and smooth, furrowing with age

Flower: pale green-to-yellow flower, ¼" (.6 cm) wide, in upright pyramidal clusters, 3–6" (7.5–15 cm) tall

Fruit: red berry-like fruit (drupe), ⅛" (.3 cm) diameter, covered with a dense coating of hairs, in cone-shaped clusters, 3–6" (7.5–15 cm) tall

Fall Color: red

Origin/Age: native; 25–50 years

Habitat: dry or poor soils, forest edges, along highways, hillsides, valleys, sun

Range: eastern quarter of Texas, planted along roadways and in parks

Stan's Notes: Small tree to large shrub, commonly seen along roads in Texas. Planted by many highway departments for its fast growth and thicket formation, stabilizing soils. It suckers readily, producing large stands of genetically identical trees. Many bird species eat the abundant fruit and deposit seeds later, starting new trees. Also called Black Sumac, and Wing-rib Sumac or Winged Sumac for its unique winged central leaf stalk (rachis).

immature fruit

bark

fruit

Bitternut Hickory
Carya cordiformis

Family: Walnut (Juglandaceae)

Height: 50–100' (15–30 m)

Tree: large tree, sturdy straight trunk, slender upright branches, open round crown

Leaf: compound, 6–10" (15–25 cm) long, alternately attached, composed of 7–11 narrow leaflets, each leaflet 3–6" (7.5–15 cm) long, with a pointed tip, fine teeth, shiny green above, paler below, lacking a leaflet stalk (sessile), attaching directly to the central stalk (rachis)

Bark: gray with irregular vertical cracks, scaly in appearance but scales are never loose

Fruit: green fruit covered with yellowish hairs, turning brown at maturity, rounded with a pointed end, ¾–1½" (2–4 cm) wide, 4 ridges on the shell

Fall Color: golden yellow

Origin/Age: native; 100–150 years

Habitat: moist, wet or loamy soils, lowlands, along rivers and streams, swamps, shade intolerant

Range: eastern quarter of Texas

Stan's Notes: Hickories grow naturally in eastern North America. About 12 species are native to North America, with 8 in Texas. The Bitternut is sometimes called Bitter Pecan because it is closely related to the familiar Pecan (pg. 339). Also called Swamp Hickory due to its preference for wet or loamy soils. Before the leaves emerge, its distinctive large yellow leaf buds are diagnostic. The wood is used to smoke meat and produces the best flavor of all hickories. Nutmeat is bitter and unpalatable to people and most wildlife. Oil extracted from the nuts was used for lamp fuel.

fruit

bark

Pignut Hickory
Carya glabra

COMPOUND
ALTERNATE

Family: Walnut (Juglandaceae)

Height: 60–80' (18–24 m)

Tree: medium to large tree, single straight trunk, bottom quarter often branch-free, short crooked branches, tips often pointing down, narrow round crown

Leaf: compound, 6–10" (15–25 cm) long, alternately attached, composed of 5 (rarely 7) lance-shaped leaflets, each leaflet 3–6" (7.5–15 cm) long, wider in the middle, with fine teeth, midrib covered with hair, yellowish green above and paler below, terminal and first pair of leaflets larger than the leaflets closest to stem, nearly stalkless

Bark: gray, becoming very shaggy with age, often peeling into long, thin, loosely attached strips

Fruit: green fruit, turning brown when mature, pear-shaped to round, 1–2" (2.5–5 cm) wide, in small clusters, thin shell splits open into 4 sections

Fall Color: yellow

Origin/Age: native; 150–200 years

Habitat: well-drained dry soils, sandy and rocky soils, hillsides, ridges and other upland sites, sun

Range: isolated and scattered in far eastern Texas

Stan's Notes: One of the most common hickories in the eastern United States, but very uncommon in Texas, restricted to only six counties. Usually in mixed stands of deciduous trees. The common name "Pignut" was given because the nuts were considered fit only for hogs. Flavor is actually highly variable, with some sweet, others bitter. Was called Broom Hickory since broom handles were made from saplings. Wood was also once used in wagon wheels.

bark

fruit

Nutmeg Hickory
Carya myristiciformis

Family: Walnut (Juglandaceae)

Height: 50–70' (15–21 m)

Tree: medium tree with a single straight trunk, narrow open crown

Leaf: compound, 6–14" (15–36 cm) long, alternately attached, made of 7–9 oval leaflets, each leaflet 3–5" (7.5–13 cm) long, pointed at the tip, narrower at the base, wider in the middle, coarsely toothed, dark green above, paler and sometimes hairy below, especially the main vein, lacking a leaflet stalk (sessile)

Bark: reddish brown, thick and smooth when young, becoming scaly with age

Fruit: green fruit covered with yellow-to-brown hairs, turning brown when mature, 1–1½" (2.5–4 cm) wide, 4–sided thin shell splits open, inner nutmeat (kernel) edible

Fall Color: bronze

Origin/Age: native; 200–400 years

Habitat: moist river bottoms, sun to partial shade

Range: scattered and isolated at the eastern edge of Texas

Stan's Notes: Very uncommon in the state, found in only a handful of counties in eastern Texas. Ranges from southern Oklahoma to Alabama, but never is abundant. Not much is known about the tree. The common and species names were given because the nut appears similar to nutmeg in size and shape. The tree produces large nut crops every 2–3 years, providing a much needed food source for wildlife. When seen in the wild it is often misidentified. When cut for commercial use it is often referred to just as Hickory or Pecan.

bark

fruit

twig pith

Shagbark Hickory
Carya ovata

Family: Walnut (Juglandaceae)

Height: 40–60' (12.2–18 m)

Tree: medium-size tree with single straight trunk and tall, narrow irregular crown

Leaf: compound, 8–14" (20–36 cm) long, alternately attached, with 5 (rarely 7) pointed leaflets, each 3–4" (7.5–10 cm) long, widest at the middle, upper 3 leaflets larger than the lower 2, fine teeth, yellowish green, lacking a leaflet stalk (sessile), attaching directly to the central stalk (rachis)

Bark: gray in color, long smooth vertical strips curling at each end, giving a shaggy appearance, large flakes or plates that easily break off

Fruit: green fruit, turning brown at maturity, nut kernel inside is sweet, edible, round to ovate, 1–1½" (2.5–4 cm) wide, single or in pairs, thick 4–ribbed husk

Fall Color: yellow

Origin/Age: native; 150–200 years

Habitat: rich moist soils, hillsides, slopes, bottomlands, sun

Range: eastern edge of Texas (Pineywoods)

Stan's Notes: The common name is for the large scaly or "shaggy" bark. Also called Shellbark, Upland Hickory, Carolina Hickory or Sealbark Hickory. Hickories are separated into two groups: true hickories, which include Shagbark, and pecan hickories such as the Bitternut Hickory (pg. 325). Shagbark nuts are eaten by wildlife and people. Wood is extremely hard and used for tool handles, skis and wagon wheels. Unlike walnut tree twigs, which have a light brown pith, Shagbark twigs have a white pith (see inset). In Texas the tree is usually alone or with one other. Never in pure stands.

bark

fruit

Water Hickory
Carya aquatica

Family: Walnut (Juglandaceae)

Height: 70–90' (21–27 m)

Tree: large tree with a single straight trunk and many slender upright branches, narrow tapered crown

Leaf: compound, 8–14" (20–36 cm) long, alternately attached, composed of 9–13 lance-shaped leaflets, each leaflet 2–5" (5–13 cm) long, curved with a pointed tip and fine-toothed margin, dark green, often covered with fine hairs below, lacks a leaflet stalk (sessile)

Bark: light brown with long fissures and thin, shaggy, sometimes red-tinged scales

Fruit: fleshy green fruit, round, 1–1½" (2.5–4 cm) wide, in clusters of 2–4, thin husk splits into quarters, releasing a hard-shelled nut, nut splits into halves

Fall Color: yellow

Origin/Age: native; 150–200 years

Habitat: wet soils, along rivers, floodplains

Range: eastern third of Texas

Stan's Notes: The Greek species name *aquatica* means "growing in water," accurately describing the habitat. One of the tallest hickories, growing only in wet soils along rivers and other wetlands. Breeds with the Pecan (pg. 339), producing hybrids. Similar to the Pecan, usually with narrower leaflets and smoother margins. Best identified by its nut husk, which is flattened, rough and has four distinct seams. Bitter nutmeat is eaten by ducks, turkeys, squirrels and other wildlife. Occasionally called Bitter Pecan or Swamp Hickory, names by which Bitternut Hickory (pg. 325) is also known. Wood is used to hickory-smoke meat such as ham and bacon.

bark

fruit

Black Hickory
Carya texana

Family: Walnut (Juglandaceae)

Height: 40–60' (12.2–18 m)

Tree: medium tree with a single straight trunk and large round spreading crown

Leaf: compound, 8–14" (20–36 cm) long, alternately attached, composed of 5–7 lance-shaped leaflets, each leaflet 2–6" (5–15 cm) long, with a fine-toothed margin, shiny dark green above, paler and sometimes with small hairs on veins below, lacks a leaflet stalk (sessile)

Bark: dark brown to nearly black, turning gray with age, thick with deep furrows and ridges

Fruit: fleshy green fruit, round, 1–1½" (2.5–4 cm) wide, thin husk splits open into 4 parts, releasing a hard-shelled nut with a small nutmeat

Fall Color: yellowish green

Origin/Age: native; 150–200 years

Habitat: wide variety of soils, wet river bottoms, dry hillsides, sandy upland sites

Range: eastern third of Texas, isolated pockets in central Texas

Stan's Notes: A true hickory that is adapted to grow in the widest variety of soil types. Found in poor soil conditions, both wet and dry, usually indicating low soil fertility, but also grows in rich soils. Tends to be slow growing due to the poor soils. Very strong wood, but not considered to be of much value because the tree does not reach a large size. Wood has been used for fence posts, tool handles and gunstocks. Fruit is eaten by squirrels, deer and other wildlife. Sometimes called Texas Hickory or Buckley Hickory.

bark

immature fruit

fruit

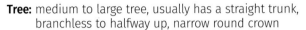

Mockernut Hickory
Carya tomentosa

Family: Walnut (Juglandaceae)

Height: 40–80' (12.2–24 m)

Tree: medium to large tree, usually has a straight trunk, branchless to halfway up, narrow round crown

Leaf: compound, 8–20" (20–50 cm) long, alternately attached, made of 7–9 leaflets, each leaflet 2–8" (5–20 cm) long, elliptical, pointed at the tip, round at the base, wider middle, fine teeth, shiny dark green above, paler and hairy below, leaflet nearly stalkless

Bark: gray to light brown with narrow forked ridges

Fruit: thick-shelled green fruit, turning brown when mature, 1½–2" (4–5 cm) wide, inner nut edible, tan to light brown, ¾–1" (2–2.5 cm) wide, 4–sided

Fall Color: yellow

Origin/Age: native; 300–500 years

Habitat: wide variety of soils, moist bottomlands, dry upland sites, sun

Range: eastern third of Texas

Stan's Notes: The most common hickory in eastern Texas and one of the tallest hickories in the state. Wood is valued for its strength for furniture; also used to smoke meat such as ham. Species name comes from the Latin *tomentum*, meaning "covered with dense short hairs," referring to the underside of leaves and helping identify the species. Also known as White Hickory due to the light color of the wood. The common name "Mockernut" comes from the large thick-shelled fruit with very small kernels of meat inside. Nuts are an important wildlife food; many birds and animals eat or store them for winter. Produces nuts after 20 years, but the prime nut-bearing age is 50–150 years. Stout hairy twigs, often reddish brown.

bark

immature fruit

fruit

Pecan

Carya illinoinensis

Family: Walnut (Juglandaceae)

Height: 80–100' (24–30 m)

Tree: large tree with a single trunk and tall, broad round crown composed of long spreading branches

Leaf: compound, 12–20" (30–50 cm) long, alternately attached, composed of 11–17 slightly curved leaflets, each leaflet 2–7" (5–18 cm) long, with a pointed tip and fine saw-toothed margin, yellowish green above, paler below

Bark: light brown and smooth, turning gray and deeply furrowed into scaly ridges with age

Fruit: green fruit, turning brown at maturity, oblong and pointed, 1–2" (2.5–5 cm) long, in clusters of 3–7, thin husk splits along 4 ridges, releasing a hard-shelled nut with a sweet, edible nutmeat (kernel)

Fall Color: yellow

Origin/Age: native; 150–300 years

Habitat: moist soils, along river valleys and floodplains, sun to partial shade

Range: eastern half of Texas, planted in parks and yards

Stan's Notes: One of the largest of hickories, sometimes growing higher than 100 feet (30 m). It is the most widespread hickory in Texas and found just about everywhere except for the Trans-Pecos region and the high plains. Improved varieties that produce thin-shelled nuts are planted in large orchards on plantations, where millions of nuts are collected and processed annually. Often planted in yards for the nuts. Latin species name *illinoensis* means "nuts from Illinois" and refers to the area where it was first described by early traders. Was an important food source for American Indians, who may have expanded its range by planting it as they relocated.

flower

bark

fruit

thorn

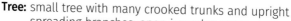

New Mexico Locust
Robinia neomexicana

Family: Pea or Bean (Fabaceae)

Height: 10–20' (3–6.1 m)

Tree: small tree with many crooked trunks and upright spreading branches, open irregular crown

Leaf: compound, 6–12" (15–30 cm) long, alternately attached, made of 12–21 oval to round leaflets, each leaflet 1½–1¾" (4–4.5 cm) long, lacks teeth, blue green, on a short leaflet stalk (petiolule)

Bark: reddish brown and rough, becoming furrowed and scaly with age, pairs of straight to curved large stout thorns, especially on twigs and branches

Flower: pea-like rose red flower, ½–1" (1–2.5 cm) long, in tight showy clusters, 2–4" (5–10 cm) long, fragrant

Fruit: flat green pod, turning brown when mature, 2–4" (5–10 cm) long, covered in fuzzy hairs, containing 3–8 seeds, pods edible, seeds toxic

Fall Color: yellow

Origin/Age: native; 75–100 years

Habitat: any soils between 5,000–8,000' (1,525–2,440 m), canyons, along streams, shade intolerant

Range: Guadalupe Mountains of the Trans-Pecos region

Stan's Notes: A tree of high elevations, often forming a dense thicket and associated with pines and oaks. Planted to control erosion since it grows fast and forms impenetrable thickets. Deer and many other large animals eat the leaves. Smaller animals depend on the plentiful seeds. Indigenous peoples ate the pods fresh or dried them for storage and used the plant medicinally for many ailments. Seeds, bark and roots are poisonous to people, but are food to many animals.

thorn

bark

flower

fruit

Black Locust
Robinia pseudoacacia

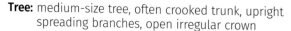

Family: Pea or Bean (Fabaceae)

Height: 30–50' (9.1–15 m)

Tree: medium-size tree, often crooked trunk, upright spreading branches, open irregular crown

Leaf: compound, 7–14" (18–36 cm) long, alternately attached, composed of 7–19 oval to round leaflets, each leaflet 1–2" (2.5–5 cm) long, toothless margin, yellowish green

Bark: dark brown and smooth, becoming furrowed and scaly with age, 2 stout thorns opposite each other at the base of leafstalk, especially on young trees

Flower: pea-like white flower with a yellow center, ½–1" (1–2.5 cm) wide, hanging in clusters, 2–4" (5–10 cm) long, appearing soon after leaves develop, fragrant

Fruit: flat green pod, turning brown when mature, 2–4" (5–10 cm) long, containing 4–8 seeds

Fall Color: yellow

Origin/Age: non-native; 75–100 years

Habitat: adapts to almost any type of soil, moist woods, shade intolerant

Range: planted along roads, in parks and around homes

Stan's Notes: Fifteen species of locust trees and shrubs, all native to North America. Wood is so strong that the British credited success of the U.S. naval fleet in the War of 1812 to the ship lumber. In Texas it is usually found only in association with people. Closely related to New Mexico Locust (pg. 341), which is native and grows in large stands in canyons and other sheltered places. Branches and twigs have pairs of thorns on leafstalks. Spreads rapidly by root suckering. Susceptible to Locust Borer beetles, which bore into trunks.

twig

bark

flower

fruit

Arizona Walnut

Juglans major

Family: Walnut (Juglandaceae)

Height: 20–40' (6.1–12.2 m)

Tree: small to medium tree, single straight or crooked trunk, open round crown

Leaf: compound, 8–14" (20–36 cm) long, alternately attached, with 9–14 stalkless leaflets (sessile), each leaflet 3–4" (7.5–10 cm) long, with a pointed tip, fine-toothed wavy edge, last (terminal) leaflet often smaller or absent, yellowish green and smooth above, slightly lighter and hairy below

Bark: brown to black, becoming darker with age, deep pits and flat scaly ridges

Flower: catkin, 4–8" (10–20 cm) long, composed of many tiny green flowers, ¼" (.6 cm) wide

Fruit: green fleshy fruit, round, 1–2" (2.5–5 cm) wide, in clusters, aromatic green husk around a hard dark nut with a sweet, edible kernel, maturing in fall

Fall Color: yellowish green

Origin/Age: native; 200–400 years

Habitat: moist soils, along streams and other wet places, canyons, river bottoms, sun to partial shade

Range: scattered in isolated pockets in central and western Texas, planted in parks and yards

Stan's Notes: A fast-growing, long-lived walnut species and one of the taller trees in western Texas. Wood doesn't shrink or warp and is used for furniture and cabinets. Twigs have a chambered pith (see inset). Pioneers used the fruit husks to dye clothes brown. Also called Nogal, Nogal Silvestre, River Walnut or Mountain Walnut. Ranges up the mountains of Mexico into Arizona, for which it is named.

bark

fruit

twig

Texas Walnut
Juglans microcarpa

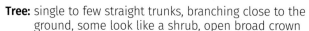

Family: Walnut (Juglandaceae)

Height: 25–50' (7.6–15 m)

Tree: single to few straight trunks, branching close to the ground, some look like a shrub, open broad crown

Leaf: compound, 8–16" (20–40 cm) long, alternately attached, with 11–25 leaflets, each 2–3" (5–7.5 cm) long, lance-shaped with an elongated pointed tip, often curved, middle leaflets larger than on ends, fine-toothed margin, yellowish green and smooth above, slightly lighter and sparsely hairy below

Bark: gray and smooth when young, dark gray to brown and becoming furrowed with flat ridges with age

Fruit: green fleshy fruit, round, 1–1½" (2.5–4 cm) wide, single or in clusters of 2–3, aromatic green husk around a hard dark nut, nutmeat sweet and edible

Fall Color: yellowish green

Origin/Age: native; 150–175 years

Habitat: moist soils, along river valleys, canyons and other moist locations, sun to partial shade

Range: scattered in central and western Texas, planted in parks and yards, sometimes planted as shelterbelts

Stan's Notes: A small walnut of Texas, sometimes appearing like a large shrub with multiple trunks. Usually in riverbeds and valleys where there is more moisture. Its large taproot reaches water that other trees cannot obtain. Twigs have a chambered pith (see inset). Occurs in pockets in Texas, Oklahoma, New Mexico and Mexico. A close relative, Arizona Walnut (pg. 345), can be hard to distinguish; may hybridize where ranges overlap. Many wildlife species depend on the small walnuts for food each fall. Also called Nogalito.

twig pith

bark

flower

fruit

Black Walnut
Juglans nigra

Family: Walnut (Juglandaceae)

Height: 50–75' (15–23 m)

Tree: single straight trunk, open round crown

Leaf: compound, 12–24" (30–60 cm) long, alternately attached, with 15–23 stalkless leaflets (sessile), each leaflet 3–4" (7.5–10 cm) long, with pointed tip, last (terminal) leaflet often smaller or absent, middle leaflets larger than on either end, fine-toothed margin, yellowish green and smooth above, slightly lighter and hairy below

Bark: brown to black, becoming darker with age, deep pits and flat scaly ridges

Flower: catkin, 2–4" (5–10 cm) long, composed of many tiny green flowers, ¼" (.6 cm) wide

Fruit: green fleshy fruit, round, 1–2" (2.5–5 cm) wide, in clusters, aromatic green husk around a hard dark nut with a sweet, edible nutmeat, maturing in fall

Fall Color: yellowish green

Origin/Age: native; 150–175 years

Habitat: well-drained rich soils, river valleys, wetlands, shade intolerant

Range: eastern quarter of Texas, planted in parks, yards

Stan's Notes: One of six walnut species native to North America. Wood doesn't shrink or warp and is used for furniture and cabinets. An important source of food for wildlife. Twigs have a brown chambered pith (see inset). Fruit husks contain a substance that stains skin; used by pioneers to dye clothing brown. Fallen leaves and roots produce juglone, a natural herbicide that prevents other trees and even its own seeds to sprout and grow beneath the adult tree.

bark

flower

fruit

Hercules Club
Zanthoxylum clava-herculis

Family: Rue (Rutaceae)

Height: 15–20' (4.6–6.1 m)

Tree: small tree with a single or multiple crooked trunks, round crown

Leaf: compound, 5–8" (13–20 cm) long, alternately attached, composed of 7–9 lance-shaped leaflets, each leaflet 1–2½" (2.5–6 cm) long, pointed, with a toothed margin, leathery, shiny green above, paler below, on a stout spiny leafstalk

Bark: light gray and thin, with many corky outgrowths tipped with short stout thorns covering the trunk and branches, often dropping thorns with age

Flower: bell-shaped light yellow-to-green flower, ¼" (.6 cm) long, in clusters

Fruit: green berry-like fruit (drupe), turning red brown at maturity, leathery, ¼" (.6 cm) wide, in clusters, splitting open in fall, with 1 seed hanging from pod

Fall Color: yellow

Origin/Age: native; 25–50 years

Habitat: variety of soils, prefers moist soils, prairies, understory of oaks, pines and sweetgum, sun to shade

Range: eastern half of Texas

Stan's Notes: Close relative of oranges and limes, also in the Rue (or Citrus) family. Occurs from Texas to Georgia and Florida. Scattered, alone and not abundant. Zanthoxylin, an oil with a citrus scent, is in the leaves and fruit. Also called Toothachetree since fruit and inner bark were used in treatment to numb the mouth. The genus name *Zanthoxylum* ("yellow wood") describes the wood color. Flowers in April and May before leaves appear. Many birds eat the fruit.

bark

cone

fruit

Western Soapberry

Sapindus saponaria drummondii

Family: Soapberry (Sapindaceae)

Height: 20–30' (6.1–9.1 m)

Tree: single trunk, sometimes with several small trunks, broad round crown

Leaf: compound, 10–17" (25–43 cm) long, alternately attached, composed of 7–19 leaflets, each 2–4" (5–10 cm) long, lacking teeth along the edge, with a pointed tip, terminal leaflet smaller than others, pale green above, lighter and slightly hairy below

Bark: gray to reddish brown and smooth, breaking into fissures with age

Flower: 5–petaled yellow-to-white flower, ¼" (.6 cm) wide, in spike clusters, 6–9" (15–23 cm) long

Fruit: green berry, turning yellow to orange to red with age, ¼–½" (.6–1 cm) wide, with a leathery skin

Fall Color: yellow

Origin/Age: native; 50–75 years

Habitat: nearly all soil types, along washes and streams, grasslands, oak woodlands, prairies, desert scrub, canyons, sun

Range: throughout Texas except the southern tip, eastern edge and parts of the panhandle

Stan's Notes: Also called Soapberry, Jaboncillo and Wild Chinatree. In Texas some grow 50 feet (15 m) tall or more. Covered with pretty flowers in spring. Although fruit stays on the tree in winter, it is not eaten by wildlife. The leathery skin of the fruit is poisonous, containing saponin, but it makes a good soap for washing. Slow-growing, not in favor with nurseries. Has great potential as an ornamental tree. Wood is dense, hard and used for tool handles and basketry.

thorn

bark

flower

fruit

Texas Ebony
Ebenopsis ebano

Family: Pea or Bean (Fabaceae)

Height: 20–30' (6.1–9.1 m)

Tree: single straight trunk with a large round crown

Leaf: twice compound, 1–2" (2.5–5 cm) long, each with 3–6 oppositely attached leaflet pairs, each leaflet 1" (2.5 cm) long, oval with a round tip, smooth margin, light green, leathery and smooth above, slightly lighter below

Bark: gray and smooth when young, dark fissures with age, pairs of stout thorns

Flower: cream-to-yellow flower, ¼" (.6 cm) wide, many flowers in dense clusters, 1–5" (2.5–13 cm) long

Fruit: large green pod, turning brown when mature, curved or straight, 4–6" (10–15 cm) long, with several reddish brown seeds, may stay on the tree until spring

Fall Color: evergreen

Origin/Age: native; 150–200 years

Habitat: sandy, rocky and clay soils, along river valleys and other moist locations, sun to partial shade

Range: southern tip of Texas, planted in parks and yards

Stan's Notes: A small tree in the far southern tip of Texas, but also planted in the southern half of the state and other warm regions such as southern Florida. A Pea family member, with edible seeds in its mature brown seed pods. Historically, Mexicans roasted the seeds and used them for a coffee substitute. Wood is heavy, close-grained and reddish, making it desirable for cabinet making. Also called Ebony Blackbead, Ebony Ape's Earring and Ebano.

thorn

bark

flower

fruit

Wright Acacia
Acacia wrightii

Family: Pea or Bean (Fabaceae)

Height: 20–30' (6.1–9.1 m)

Tree: single crooked or multiple trunks with multiple branching, broad irregular crown

Leaf: twice compound, 1–2" (2.5–5 cm) long, alternately attached, with 2–8 pairs of leaflet stalks along each side of central stalk (rachis), each with 6–12 tiny oblong leaflets, each ¼" (.6 cm) long, soft green above, paler below, stalkless (sessile)

Bark: gray, thin and smooth when young, turning brown with narrow scales with age, stout thorns on twigs

Flower: yellow flower, ¼" (.6 cm) long, in elongated spikes, ¾–1½" (2–4 cm) tall, located at the base of leaves, fragrant

Fruit: large pea-like green pod, turning dark reddish brown at maturity, slightly curved, 2–6" (5–15 cm) long and up to 1¼" (3 cm) diameter, with several flattened edible seeds

Fall Color: semi-evergreen

Origin/Age: native; 25–50 years

Habitat: rocky and sandy soils, slopes, canyons, along washes and streams, sun

Range: scattered in western, central and southern Texas

Stan's Notes: A drought-tolerant small tree when near water, shrub-like in dry habitats. Often forms thickets, where many bird species take refuge. Ranges from northern Mexico into Texas. Seeds are eaten by quail, nearly all small animals and people. Its hard wood makes good firewood and fence posts. Bees produce a tasty honey from its flowers. Excellent for landscaping due to the handsome flowers.

thorn

bark

flower

fruit

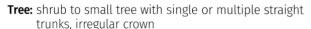

Catclaw Acacia
Acacia greggii

Family: Pea or Bean (Fabaceae)

Height: 10–20' (3–6.1 m)

Tree: shrub to small tree with single or multiple straight trunks, irregular crown

Leaf: twice compound, 2–3" (5–7.5 cm) long, alternately attached, with 2–3 pairs of leaflet stalks along each side of central stalk (rachis), each stalk with 8–12 leaflets, each leaflet ¼" (.6 cm) long, widest above the middle, grayish green, on a short leaflet stalk

Bark: gray and smooth, turning brown and scaly

Flower: yellow-to-white flower, ⅛" (.3 cm) long, in round or elongated clusters, ¾–2" (2–5 cm) long

Fruit: large pea-like green pod, turning reddish with age, then brown, twisted, wrinkly, 2–5" (5–13 cm) long

Fall Color: semi-evergreen

Origin/Age: native; 25–50 years

Habitat: rocky and sandy soils, canyons, deserts, washes, streams, sun

Range: southwestern Texas from the Trans-Pecos to the Rio Grande Valley

Stan's Notes: Also called Wait-a-minute-tree, Paradiseflower, Gregg Catclaw or Devil's Claw. Most names refer to its hooked thorns, the size and shape of cat claws. These hook passers-by, tearing clothes. Often forms a thicket, sheltering wildlife. Lacks leaves most of the year, which conserves water. Sprouts leaves after monsoons. Leaves and flowers are similar to mesquite, but catclaw thorns are broad at the base and curve back; mesquite thorns are straight. Catclaw pods split open at maturity; mesquite pods do not. Species *greggii* refers to Josiah Gregg, a naturalist explorer of the Southwest and Mexico.

thorn

bark

flower

fruit

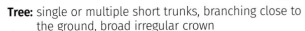
Roemer Acacia

Acacia roemeriana

Family: Pea or Bean (Fabaceae)

Height: 10–20' (3–6.1 m)

Tree: single or multiple short trunks, branching close to the ground, broad irregular crown

Leaf: twice compound, 2–3" (5–7.5 cm) long, alternately attached, with 2–8 pairs of leaflet stalks along each side of central stalk (rachis), each with 4–12 tiny leaflets, each ¼" (.6 cm) long, bright green, on a short leaflet stalk (petiolule)

Bark: gray and smooth, turning brown and scaly with age, pairs of stout thorns on twigs

Flower: whitish yellow flower, ¼" (.6 cm) long, in round (ball) clusters, ¾" (2 cm) wide, located at the base of leaves, fragrant

Fruit: large pea-like green pod, turning dark reddish purple to brown, leathery and flexible at maturity, 2–4" (5–10 cm) long and up to 1¼" (3 cm) wide, containing several flattened edible seeds

Fall Color: semi-evergreen

Origin/Age: native; 25–50 years

Habitat: rocky and sandy soils, slopes, bluffs, canyons, deserts, along washes and streams, sun

Range: scattered in west central Texas

Stan's Notes: A shrub to small tree, often forming thickets. More tree-like when near water. Ranges from northern Mexico into Texas. Named for Karl Ferdinand Roemer (1818–91) of Germany, who collected and described this plant in Texas in 1846. Seeds are eaten by wildlife and people. Wood is hard, making good firewood. This acacia and all others are Mimosoideae subfamily members.

flower

bark

fruit

thorn

Sweet Acacia
Vachellia farnesiana

Family: Pea or Bean (Fabaceae)

Height: 10–20' (3–6.1 m)

Tree: single or multiple short trunks, branching close to the ground, broad irregular crown

Leaf: twice compound, 2–3" (5–7.5 cm) long, alternately attached, with 2–8 pairs of leaflet stalks along each side of central stalk (rachis), each with 12–24 tiny leaflets, each ¼" (.6 cm) long, asymmetrical base, bright green, on a short leaflet stalk (petiolule)

Bark: gray and smooth, turning brown and scaly with age, pairs of stout thorns on twigs

Flower: lemon yellow flower, ⅛" (.3 cm) long, in round (ball) clusters, ¾–1" (2–2.5 cm) wide, fragrant

Fruit: large pea-like green pod, turning dark reddish purple to brown and woody when mature, 2–3" (5–7.5 cm) long, several thick, shiny edible seeds

Fall Color: semi-evergreen

Origin/Age: native; 25–50 years

Habitat: rocky and sandy soils, slopes, canyons, deserts, along washes and streams, sun

Range: southern third of Texas

Stan's Notes: A handsome species when covered in its yellow puff-ball blooms. Flowers have a scent reminiscent of candy. Native range is in Mexico and Central America, reaching its northern limits in southern Texas. An evergreen if there is enough water; drops leaves otherwise. Seeds are consumed by wildlife and have been a food for people around the world. Wood is hard and makes good firewood. The species name is from the Farnese Gardens in Rome. Also called Texas Huisache, Huisache or Cassie.

bark

flower

fruit

Goldenball Leadtree
Leucaena retusa

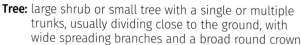

Family: Pea or Bean (Fabaceae)

Height: 20–25' (6.1–7.6 m)

Tree: large shrub or small tree with a single or multiple trunks, usually dividing close to the ground, with wide spreading branches and a broad round crown

Leaf: twice compound, 3–8" (7.5–20 cm) long, alternately attached, with 2–4 pairs of stalks, each with 3–8 pairs of leaflets, each ⅓–1" (.8–2.5 cm) long, curved, pointed, with a smooth edge, bright green

Bark: gray to cinnamon brown and thin, becoming flaky with age

Flower: 5–petaled yellow flower, ⅛" (.3 cm) long, many flowers in round clusters, 1–1¼" (2.5–3 cm) wide, on a long stalk

Fruit: green pod, turning brown when mature, curved, flattened, thin and papery, 3–10" (7.5–25 cm) long, containing many small shiny seeds

Fall Color: semi-evergreen

Origin/Age: native; 50–150 years

Habitat: dry rocky and sandy soils, sun

Range: central and western Texas including the Trans-Pecos, planted in parks and yards across the state

Stan's Notes: A pretty tree with bright leaves, cinnamon branches and clusters of yellow flowers. Flowers bloom in midspring and after rain in summer and fall. The *Leucaena* genus has 40–50 species in Central and South America and the West Indies, with only 3 in the United States and a few non-native species introduced as landscape trees. Grazed by cattle and wildlife. Many bird species eat the seeds. Also called Lemonball, Littleleaf Leadtree and Wahootree.

bark

flower

Great Leadtree
Leucaena pulverulenta

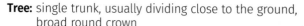

Family: Pea or Bean (Fabaceae)

Height: 25–50' (7.6–15 m)

Tree: single trunk, usually dividing close to the ground, broad round crown

Leaf: twice compound, 4–10" (10–25 cm) long, alternately attached, with 14–20 pairs of stalks, each with 15–40 pairs of leaflets, each ⅓" (.8 cm) long, with a smooth edge, feathery and bright green

Bark: gray to cinnamon brown and thin, becoming flaky with age

Flower: 5–petaled white flower, ⅛" (.3 cm) long, many flowers in round clusters, 1" (2.5 cm) wide, on a long stalk rising from the leaf attachment, fragrant

Fruit: green pod, turning brown when mature, straight, flattened with thickened edges, 4–12" (10–30 cm) long, containing several small shiny seeds

Fall Color: semi-evergreen

Origin/Age: native; 50–150 years

Habitat: wet soils, moist soils, along streams and other wet locations, sun

Range: southern tip of Texas, planted in parks and yards throughout the state

Stan's Notes: Often grows as a wide shrub, but can be a large tree when growing in moist soils. Flowers in spring and summer. The sweet blossoms and large feathery leaves make it an attractive tree for landscapes. Not cold tolerant; does not do well above the lower Rio Grande Valley. Natural range is from central Mexico, reaching its northern limits in Texas. Wood is hard and heavy, but not used commercially. Also called Mexican Leadtree or Tepeguaje.

bark

flower

fruit

White Leadtree
Leucaena leucocephala

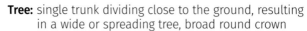

Family: Pea or Bean (Fabaceae)

Height: 10–20' (3–6.1 m)

Tree: single trunk dividing close to the ground, resulting in a wide or spreading tree, broad round crown

Leaf: twice compound, 4–12" (10–30 cm) long, alternately attached, with 2–4 pairs of stalks, each with 10–20 pairs of small leaflets, each leaflet ⅜–½" (.9–1 cm) long, curved and pointed, with a smooth edge (margin), yellow green

Bark: gray to reddish brown and thin, developing ridges and scales with age

Flower: 5–petaled white flower, ⅛" (.3 cm) long, in ball clusters, 1–1¼" (2.5–3 cm) wide, on a long stalk

Fruit: green pod, turning brown when mature, straight or twisted, flattened and thicker on edges, 3–6" (7.5–15 cm) long, on a short fruit stalk, with many flattened, edible shiny seeds

Fall Color: semi-evergreen

Origin/Age: non-native; 50–150 years

Habitat: dry rocky and sandy soils, sun

Range: scattered throughout the southern half of Texas

Stan's Notes: A thornless tree that grows quickly, naturalizing itself wherever seeds are cast. Also called Wild Tamarind, Jumby Bean, Leadtree or Lamtoro. Native to Mexico and Central America, it has been introduced to places around the world and become a serious nuisance. Planted as a food tree for people and animals, it has taken over and pushed out many native plants. High-protein leaves are fed to cattle. People and livestock eat the seeds. Used for firewood, windbreaks, and for shade in third-world country coffee crops.

thorn on trunk

bark

fruit

thorn

Water Locust
Gleditsia aquatica

Family: Pea or Bean (Fabaceae)

Height: 30–50' (9.1–15 m)

Tree: medium-size tree with a short trunk divided low, broad flat-topped crown

Leaf: twice compound (sometimes compound), 4–8" (10–20 cm) long, alternately attached, composed of 15–30 oblong leaflets, each leaflet ½–1¼" (1–3 cm) long, with a wavy margin, shiny dark green above, much duller below, stalkless (sessile)

Bark: brown to gray, thin and smooth, becoming scaly with age, with thorns on branches and many large branched thorns on trunk

Flower: 5–petaled green flower, ¼" (.6 cm) wide, in clusters up to 4" (10 cm) long

Fruit: large pea-like green pod, flat, turning brown and papery at maturity, 1–2" (2.5–5 cm) long, hanging in clusters, containing 1 large flattened seed

Fall Color: yellow

Origin/Age: native; 100–125 years

Habitat: wet soils, along wetlands and rivers, shade to sun

Range: eastern edge in the Pineywoods, Gulf Prairies and Marshes

Stan's Notes: A smaller version of the Honey Locust (pg. 373), with smaller leaves and pulpless pods. The common name "Water" is for its habit of growing in wet areas. Species name *aquatica* also refers to its water-loving nature. Not a favorite tree for planting in parks and yards because of its thorny branches and large clusters of thorns on its trunk. Wood is heavy, strong and hard and has been used for tool handles and fence posts.

bark

flower

fruit

Honey Locust
Gleditsia triacanthos

Family: Pea or Bean (Fabaceae)

Height: 40–60' (12.2–18 m)

Tree: single trunk, often divided low, open broad crown, sometimes flat-topped

Leaf: twice compound, 12–24" (30–61 cm) long, alternately attached, composed of 14–30 elliptical, feathery leaflets, each leaflet 1" (2.5 cm) long, fine teeth, dark green above, yellow green below

Bark: reddish brown covered with gray horizontal lines (lenticels), often cracking and peeling, frequently thorny on trunk and branches

Flower: small green catkin, 1–2" (2.5–5 cm) long

Fruit: large pea-like purplish brown pod, flat, twisted, 6–16" (15–40 cm) long, 12–14 oval seeds per pod

Fall Color: yellow

Origin/Age: native; 100–125 years

Habitat: moist or rich soils, sun

Range: eastern third of Texas except the far south, planted in parks, yards and along roads

Stan's Notes: Also called Thorny Locust because it has large thorns on the trunk and branches and twigs are zigzagged with thorns at joints. Between seeds in seedpods is a sweet yellowish substance, hence "Honey" in the common name. Seedpods are large, obvious and eaten by wildlife. Should not be pruned in wet weather since it opens the tree to infection by Nectria canker. Thornless and seedless varieties are widely planted in parks and yards and along roads. Most varieties planted in landscaping lack thorns and fruit. Largest of the two species of *Gleditsia* native to North America.

bark

fruit

Chinaberry
Melia azedarach

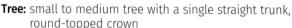

Family: Mahogany (Meliaceae)

Height: 20–40' (6.1–12.2 m)

Tree: small to medium tree with a single straight trunk, round-topped crown

Leaf: twice compound, 8–16" (20–40 cm) long, alternately attached, composed of many lance-shaped leaflets, each leaflet 1–3" (2.5–7.5 cm) long, with a pointed tip and many sharp teeth, bright green

Bark: reddish brown, thin and smooth when young, becoming furrowed with age

Flower: lavender-to-purple flower, ¼–½" (.6–1 cm) wide, made of 5 narrow swept-back petals, many flowers on a few upright stalks, smells like grape Kool-Aid

Fruit: round green capsule (drupe), turning yellow with age, ¼–½" (.6–1 cm) wide, toxic

Fall Color: yellow

Origin/Age: non-native, introduced from Asia; 100–125 years

Habitat: rocky and sandy soils, sun

Range: planted in parks and yards throughout Texas

Stan's Notes: Originates from the Himalayas. An ornamental in the Southwest and southern states. Birds and animals that eat the fruit transport the seeds into the wild, where the tree has established and is now naturalized in many places. In many states it is considered a noxious weed. Fast growing and short lived, covered with attractive lavender flowers in spring and yellow fruit at the end of summer. Fruit is poisonous to people and livestock and may cause trouble to birds if too many are eaten. Also called Chinatree, Persian Lilac, Tulipcedar or Chinaballtree. The species name *azedarach* is from the Persian *azad*, meaning "noble," and *darakh* for "tree."

fruit

flower

bark

Silktree
Albizia julibrissin

Family: Pea or Bean (Fabaceae)

Height: 20–30' (6.1–9.1 m)

Tree: single or multi-trunk tree, long arching branches, large round crown

Leaf: twice compound, 10–16" (25–40 cm) long, alternately attached, composed of a central stalk (rachis) with 6–16 smaller stalks, each with 18–30 pairs of leaflets, each ½–¾" (1–2 cm) long, thin, feathery, with a smooth margin, yellow green

Bark: dark greenish brown, thin and smooth, turning darker with vertical stripes with age

Flower: fuzzy, pink-tipped, white tubular flower, ⅛" (.3 cm) wide, in clusters, 1–3" (2.5–7.5 cm) long

Fruit: pea-like green pod, turning tan when mature, straight with a pointed tip, 3–8" (7.5–20 cm) long

Fall Color: semi-evergreen

Origin/Age: non-native, introduced from Asia; 25–75 years

Habitat: rocky and sandy soils, deserts, foothills, slopes, sun

Range: planted throughout Texas in gardens, patios, yards and parks

Stan's Notes: Many people love the fragrant flowers and attractive foliage of this tree. Genus is named after Filippo degli Albizzi, who introduced the tree to Europe in the mid-1700s. Species *julibrissin* is from the Persian word *Gul-i-Abrisham* for "the silk flower." Also called Persian Silktree, Mimosa Silktree and Mimosa. Many hummingbird, butterfly and honeybee species visit the flowers, which bloom in midsummer. Seeds are eaten and carried off by wildlife, allowing the tree to become established and compete with native trees.

thorn

bark

flower

fruit

Devil's Walkingstick

Aralia spinosa

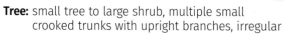

Family: Ginseng (Araliaceae)

Height: 20–30' (6.1–9.1 m)

Tree: small tree to large shrub, multiple small crooked trunks with upright branches, irregular to round crown

Leaf: twice compound, 13–36" (33–91 cm) long, alternately attached, composed of numerous leaflets, each leaflet 2–3½" (5–9 cm) long, with a pointed tip and toothed margin, dark green above, paler below with prickles on midrib

Bark: dark brown, thin fissures, scattered stout thorns

Flower: 5-petaled white-to-cream flower, ⅛" (.3 cm) wide, upright in large clusters, 8–16" (20–40 cm) long

Fruit: green berry, turning purplish when mature, ⅛–¼" (.3–.6 cm) wide, juicy and aromatic when ripe, in large clusters, containing 3–5 seeds

Fall Color: yellow

Origin/Age: native; 25–30 years

Habitat: moist soils, by streams, forest edges, shade tolerant

Range: eastern edge of Texas, Pineywoods

Stan's Notes: The Ginseng family includes more than 800 species of trees and shrubs. These are found all over the world, particularly in tropical areas. Devil's Walkingstick, planted long ago in Victorian gardens as an ornamental shrub, produces eye-catching clusters of flowers and purplish mature fruit. Its roots and fruit are extremely fragrant and were once used to cure ailments such as toothaches. Also called Angelicatree or Hercules Club, the latter common name for the short thorns growing on its bark, resembling the spiked club of the ancient Greek mythical hero.

bark

flower

fruit

Red Buckeye
Aesculus pavia

Family: Horsechestnut (Hippocastanaceae)

Height: 20–30' (6.1–9.1 m)

Tree: small tree, single straight trunk and many crooked branches, broad round crown with a flat top

Leaf: palmate compound, 5–12" (13–30 cm) long, oppositely attached, made of 5 (sometimes 7) leaflets, each leaflet 3–6" (7.5–15 cm) long, radiating from a central point, with fine irregular teeth, dark green and shiny above, pale and sometimes with white hairs below, lacking a leaflet stalk (sessile)

Bark: dark gray to brown, smooth, cracking with age

Flower: scarlet red (sometimes yellow and red) tubular flower, ½" (1 cm) in diameter, growing upright in triangular clusters, 4–8" (10–20 cm) long

Fruit: light brown smooth capsule, round, 1–2" (2.5–5 cm) wide, 1–2 shiny brown poisonous seeds

Fall Color: yellow

Origin/Age: native; 100–125 years

Habitat: moist and wet soils, river bottoms, along streams, creeks and other wet habitats, sun to partial shade

Range: eastern quarter of Texas, planted in parks, yards and along streets

Stan's Notes: Range is from Georgia and Florida to eastern Texas. Considered an understory tree, growing in the shade of larger trees. May be associated with oaks and pines. A fast-growing, short-lived tree, often flowering early in life when only a few feet tall. The three-parted fruit husk splits open in a slit that resembles the eye of a deer, hence "Buckeye" in the common name. The pretty flowers make it popular in landscapes, along with its many cultivated varieties.

flower

bark

fruit

Texas Buckeye
Aesculus glabra arguta

Family: Horsechestnut (Hippocastanaceae)

Height: 20–40' (6.1–12.2 m)

Tree: small to medium tree with a single straight trunk, broad round crown with a flat top

Leaf: palmate compound, 5–15" (13–38 cm) long, oppositely attached, made of 7–9 leaflets, each 3–5" (7.5–13 cm) long, radiating from a central point, with fine irregular teeth, yellowish green above, pale and hairy below, lacking a leaflet stalk (sessile)

Bark: brown with scaly patches, rough shallow furrows

Flower: yellow-to-green flower, ½" (1 cm) wide, growing upright in triangular clusters, 5–7" (13–18 cm) long, foul odor when crushed

Fruit: light brown spiny capsule, round, 1–2" (2.5–5 cm) wide, contains 1–2 shiny brown poisonous seeds

Fall Color: yellow to orange

Origin/Age: native; 100–125 years

Habitat: sandy soils, open woodlands, river bottoms, sun to partial shade

Range: northeastern quarter of Texas with a narrow finger reaching into central Texas, planted in landscapes

Stan's Notes: This tree has an interesting palmate leaf, with leaflets lacking their own leafstalks, all rising instead from a central stalk. In Texas considered to be a subspecies of Ohio Buckeye (not shown), differing by leaflet number and flower color. Called Fetid Buckeye or Stinking Buckeye for the foul odor of crushed parts of the tree. A mostly poisonous tree including its large seeds, which wildlife avoid. Young leaves have killed cattle when other greenery was unavailable. Often loses all leaves by midsummer due to fungal diseases.

The large cacti, palms and shrubby plants included in this special section will help you identify 6 species in Texas that superficially appear like trees, but are not. All of these species lack bark and some lack leaves. Some are native plants and can be seen growing in the wild. Others are non-native and have been planted in parks and landscapes. All are found throughout the state.

SPANISH DAGGER
Yucca treculeana
10–15'

TORREY YUCCA
Yucca torreyi
20–25'

SOAPTREE YUCCA
Yucca elata
20–30'

GIANT DAGGER
Yucca faxoniana
20–30'

SABAL PALM
Sabal mexicana
40–50'

CALIFORNIA FAN PALM
Washingtonia filifera
40–60'

GLOSSARY

Acorn: A nut, typically of oak trees, as in the Gambel Oak. See *nut* and *fruit*.

Aggregate fruit: A fruit composed of multiple tiny berries, such as a mulberry, raspberry or blackberry. See *fruit*.

Alternate: A type of leaf attachment in which the leaves are singly and alternately attached along a stalk, as in Quaking Aspen.

Arcuate: Curved in form, like a bow, as in the veins of Flowering Dogwood leaves.

Asymmetrical leaf base: A base of a leaf with lobes unequal in size or shape, as in elms. See *leaf base*.

Berry: A fleshy fruit with several seeds within, such as Texas Persimmon. See *fruit*.

Bract: A petal-like structure on a flower, as in Flowering Dogwood.

Branch: The smaller, thinner, woody parts of a tree, usually bearing the leaves and flowers.

Bristle-tipped: A type of leaf lobe ending in a projection, usually a sharply pointed tip.

Buttress: A wide or flared base of a tree trunk that helps to hold the tree upright in unstable soils, as in Bald Cypress.

Capsule: A dry fruit that opens along several seams to release the seeds within, as in Rio Grande Cottonwood. See *pod*.

Catkin: A scaly cluster of usually same sex flowers, as in Quaking Aspen or any willow.

Chambered pith: The central soft part of a twig that is broken into spaced sections, as in Black Walnut. See *pith*.

Chaparral: Deep-rooted, mostly evergreen plants that easily grow after fires.

Clasping: A type of leaf attachment without a leafstalk in which the leaf base grasps the main stalk, partly surrounding the stalk at the point of attachment.

Clustered needles: A group of needles emanating from a central point, usually within a papery sheath, as in pine trees.

Compound leaf: A single leaf composed of at least 2 but usually not more than 20 leaflets growing along a single leafstalk, as in Texas Ash.

Cone: A cluster of woody scales encasing multiple nutlets or seeds and growing on a central stalk, as in coniferous trees.

Cone scale: An individual overlapping projection, often woody, on a cone, as in Southwestern White Pine.

Conifer: A type of tree that usually does not shed all of its leaves each autumn, such as pine or spruce.

Crooked: Off center or bent in form, not straight, as in a Black Locust trunk.

Deciduous: A type of tree that usually sheds all of its leaves each autumn, such as Black Tupelo.

Dioecious: A type of tree that has male and female flowers on separate trees of the same species, as in the Quaking Aspen. See *monoecious*.

Disk: A flattened, disk-like fruit that contains a seed, as in the American Elm: See *samara*.

Double-toothed margin: A jagged or serrated leaf edge that is composed of two types of teeth, usually one small and one large, as in Siberian Elm.

Drupe: A fleshy fruit that usually has a single seed, such as a cherry. See *fruit*.

Evergreen: A plant that retains its needles or leaves all year. Leaves may persist on a tree from a few months to many years before being replaced. Many deciduous species that normally drop leaves each year, such as Gray Oak, retain them year-round in Texas. See *semi-evergreen*.

Flower: To bloom, or produce a flower or flowers as a means of reproduction, as in deciduous trees.

Fruit: A ripened ovary or reproductive structure that contains one or more seeds, such as a nut or berry.

Furrowed: Having longitudinal channels or grooves, as in Alligator Juniper bark.

Gall: An abnormal growth of plant tissue that is usually caused by insects, microorganisms or injury.

Gland: An organ or structure that secretes a substance, as in Honey Mesquite flowers.

Intolerant: Won't thrive in a particular condition, such as shade.

Lance-shaped: Long, narrow and pointed in form, like a spear-head, as in Desert Willow leaves.

Leaf base: The area where a leafstalk attaches to the leaf.

Leaflet: One of the two or more leaf-like parts of a compound leaf, as in Velvet Ash.

Leafstalk: The stalk of a leaf, extending from the leaf base to the branch. See *petiole*.

Lenticel: A small growth, usually on bark, that allows air into the interior of a tree, as in Honey Locust.

Lobed leaf: A single leaf with at least one indentation (sinus or notch) along an edge that does not reach the center or base of the leaf, as in oaks or maples.

Margin: The edge of a leaf.

Mesa: An elevated, flat expanse of land (plateau), with one or more steep sides or cliffs; Spanish for "tableland."

Midrib: The central vein of a leaf, often more pronounced and larger in size than other veins, as in Black Cherry.

Monoecious: A type of tree that has male and female flowers on the same tree, as in Gambel Oak. See *dioecious*.

Naturalized: Not originally native, growing and reproducing in the wild freely now, such as Russian Olive.

Needle: A long, usually thin, evergreen leaf of a conifer.

Notch: A small indentation along the margin of a leaf, as in Bigtooth Maple.

Nut: A large fruit encased by hard walls, usually containing one seed, such as an acorn. See *fruit*.

Nutlet: A small or diminutive nut or seed, usually contained in a cone or cone-like seed catkin, as in River Birch. See *fruit*.

Obovate: Shaped like an egg and flat, as in Pawpaw leaves.

Opposite: A type of leaf attachment in which leaves are situated directly across from each other on a stalk, as in Bigtooth Maple.

Ovate: Shaped like an egg, as in Loblolly Pine cones.

Palmate compound leaf: A single leaf that is composed of three or more leaflets emanating from a common central point at the end of the leafstalk, as in Texas Buckeye.

Petiole: The stalk of a leaf. See *leafstalk*.

Petiolule: The stalk of a leaflet in a compound leaf.

Photosynthesis: In green plants, the conversion of water and carbon dioxide from energy in sunlight into carbohydrates (food).

Pitch pocket: A raised blister that contains a thick resinous sap, as in Douglas Fir bark.

Pith: The central soft part of a twig in a young branch, turning to hard wood when mature.

Pod: A dry fruit that contains many seeds and opens at maturity, as in New Mexico Locust. See *capsule*.

Pollination: The transfer of pollen from the male anther to the female stigma, usually resulting in the production of seeds.

Pome: A fleshy fruit with several chambers that contain many seeds, such as an apple. See *fruit*.

Rachis: The central or main stalk of a compound leaf, as in the Honey Mesquite.

Samara: A winged fruit that contains a seed, as in maples, ashes or elms. See *disk* and *fruit*.

Seed catkin: A small cone-like structure that contains nutlets or seeds, as in cottonwoods.

Semi-evergreen: A plant that usually retains its leaves all year, but drops its leaves when air temperatures drop below freezing or when drought persists, such as Emory Oak. See *evergreen*.

Sessile: Lacking a stalk and attaching directly at the base, as in Bitternut Hickory leaflets.

Simple leaf: A single leaf with an undivided or unlobed edge, as in American Elm.

Sinus: The recess or space in between two lobes of a leaf, as in the Emory Oak.

Spine: A stiff, usually short, sharply pointed woody outgrowth from a branch or cone, as in Ponderosa Pine cones. See *thorn*.

Stalk: A thin structure that attaches a leaf, flower or fruit to a twig or branch.

Stipule: An appendage at the base of a stalk, usually small and in pairs, with one stipule on each side of the stalk.

Sucker: A secondary shoot produced from the base or roots of a tree that gives rise to a new plant, as in Quaking Aspen.

Tannin: A bitter-tasting chemical found within acorns and other parts of a tree, as in oaks.

Taproot: The primary, vertically descending root of a mature tree.

Terminal: Growing at the end of a stalk or branch.

Thorn: A stiff, usually long and sharply pointed woody outgrowth from a branch or trunk, as in Texas Ebony. See *spine*.

Tolerant: Will thrive in a particular condition, such as shade.

Understory: The small trees and other plants that grow under a canopy of larger trees; the shady habitat in a forest.

Wash: A usually dry and sandy streambed in the Southwest over which water flows during or after heavy rains.

Whorl: A ring of three or more leaves, stalks or branches arising from a common point, as in Southern Catalpa.

Winged: Having membranous, thin appendages, usually attached to a seed, as in maple seeds.

Woody: Composed of wood, as in trees or cones. See *cone scale*.

CHECKLIST/INDEX
Use the boxes to check trees you've seen.

393

PHOTO CREDITS *(continued from page 4)*

Will Cook: 54 (Southern Redcedar), 72 (main), 78 (all), 80 (flower), 104 (flower, fruit & main), 106 (fruit & main), 110 (flower), 124 (flower, fruit & main), 140 (flower), 168 (bark & main), 176 (all), 190 (fruit), 192 (bark), 222 (main), 242 (flower), 244 (flower & main), 160 (bark & main), 282 (fruit), 304 (fruit), 322 (flower), 328 (bark & main), 332 (fruit), 350 (bark, fruit & main), 378 (flower), 380 (flower); **Shirley Denton:** 120 (fruit), 182 (flower); **Dudley Edmondson:** 82 (bark, flower, fruit & main), 114 (bark & main), 132 (bark), 134 (bark, fruit & main), 214 (flower), 254 (bark, flower & main); **Chris Evans/River to River CWMA:** 120 (main), 166 (both), 174 (main), 240 (bark & main), 244 (bark), 260 (fruit), 332 (bark & main); **Troy Evans/Great Smoky Mountains National Park:** 370 (fruit); **James D. Flood:** 382 (bark & fruit); **Michael P. Gadomski/Dembinsky Photo Associates:** 326 (main); **Howard Garrett:** 156 (main); **Denny Girard:** 350 (flower); **Mike Haddock:** 382 (main); **Carl Hunter/USDA-NRCS PLANTS Database:** 328 (fruit); **Jerry and Barbara Jividen:** 326 (bark); **Larry Korhnak:** 72 (main), 74 (cone), 104 (bark), 124 (bark), 174 (bark & fruit), 244 (fruit); **Nikolay Kurzenko/Shutterstock.com:** 256 (flower); **Melody Lytle:** 232 (fruit), 320 (fruit); **Bruce MacQueen/Shutterstock.com:** 224 (flower); **Jim Manhart, Ph.D.:** 188 (fruit), 222 (fruit), 360 (flower); **Joseph A. Marcus/Lady Bird Johnson Wildflower Center:** 188 (flower), 220 (flower); **Fred Nation:** 116 (fruit, main & flower); **Puffin's Pictures/Shutterstock.com:** 218 (flower); **Clarence A. Rechenthin@USDA-NRCS PLANTS Database:** 292, 318 (flower); **John Ruter/University of Georgia:** 240 (immature fruit), 304 (flower); **Samuel Roberts Nobel Foundation:** 334 (all); **Al Schneider:** 206 (both); **John Seiler:** 106 (bark), 116 (bark), 120 (bark); **Andy and Sally Wasowski/Lady Bird Johnson Wildflower Center:** 80 (fruit), 154 (main), 320 (flower); and **Lisa Wylie:** 308 (flower).

The following Bugwood (weedimages.org) images below are licensed under the Creative Commons Attribution 3.0 (CC BY 3.0 US) License, available here: https://creativecommons.org/licenses/by/3.0/deed.en.

Ted Bodner/Southern Weed Science Society: 322 (fruit); **Franklin Bonner/USFS (ret.):** 168 (fruit), 180 (fruit), 272 (fruit); **Charles T. Bryson/USDA Agricultural Research Service:** 86 (flower); **Bill Cook/Michigan State University:** 250 (flower); **James H. Miller & Ted Bodner/Southern Weed Science Society:** 378 (fruit); **Pennsylvania Department of Conservation and Natural Resources/Forestry:** 254 (fruit); and **Dave Powell/USDA Forest Service:** 218 (Plains Cottonwood).

NOTES

MORE FOR TEXAS BY STAN TEKIELA

Identification Guides

Birds of Prey of the South
Field Guide

Birds of Texas Field Guide

Birds of the South

Birds of the Southwest

Catcus of Texas Field Guide

Mammals of Texas Field Guide

Shorebirds of the Southeast
& Gulf States

Stan Tekiela's Birding for
Beginners: South

Stan Tekiela's Birding for
Beginners: Southwest

Wildflowers of Texas Field Guide

Children's Books: Adventure Board Book Series

Floppers & Loppers

Paws & Claws

Peepers & Peekers

Snouts & Sniffers

Children's Books

C is for Cardinal

Can You Count the Critters?

Critter Litter

Critter Litter Southwest

The Kids' Guide to Birds of Texas

Children's Books: Wildlife Picture Books

Baby Bear Discovers the World

The Cutest Critter

Do Beavers Need Blankets?

Hidden Critters

Jump, Little Wood Ducks

Some Babies Are Wild

Super Animal Powers

What Eats That?

Whose Baby Butt?

Whose Butt?

Whose House Is That?

Whose Track Is That?

Favorite Wildlife

Backyard Birds
Bald Eagles
Bears
Bird Migration
Cranes, Herons & Egrets
Deer, Elk & Moose
Hummingbirds
Intriguing Owls
Loons
Wild Birds

Our Love of Wildlife

Our Love of Loons
Our Love of Owls

Nature Appreciation Series

Bird Nests
Feathers
Wildflowers

Nature Books

Bird Trivia
Start Mushrooming
A Year in Nature with Stan Tekiela

Nature's Wild Cards (playing cards)

Bears
Birds of the Gulf Coast
Birds of the Southwest
Hummingbirds
Loons
Mammals of the Gulf Coast
Mammals of the Southwest
Owls
Raptors
Trees of the Gulf Coast
Trees of the Southwest

ABOUT THE AUTHOR

Naturalist, wildlife photographer and writer **Stan Tekiela** is the originator of the popular state-specific field guide series that includes *Birds of Texas Field Guide*. Stan has authored more than 190 educational books, including field guides, quick guides, nature books, children's books, playing cards and more, presenting many species of animals and plants.

With a Bachelor of Science degree in Natural History from the University of Minnesota and as an active professional naturalist for more than 30 years, Stan studies and photographs wildlife throughout the United States and Canada. He has received various national and regional awards for his books and photographs. Also a well-known columnist and radio personality, he has a syndicated column that appears in more than 25 newspapers, and his wildlife programs are broadcast on a number of Midwest radio stations. Stan can be followed on Facebook and Twitter. He can be contacted via www.naturesmart.com.